Social Problems of the North

Charles E. B. Russell

Garland Publishing, Inc.
New York & London
1980

For a complete list of the titles in this series,
see the final pages of this volume.

The volumes in this series are printed on acid-free,
250-year-life paper.

This facsimile has been made from a copy in
the British Library.

Library of Congress Cataloging in Publication Data

Russell, Charles Edward Bellyse, 1866– 1917.
Social problems of the north.

(The English working class)
Reprint of the 1913 ed. published by A. R. Mowbray,
London, in series: Christian social union handbooks.
Includes index.
1. Newcastle-upon-Tyne — Social conditions.
2. Labor and laboring-classes — England — Case studies.
3. England — Poor — Case studies.
4. Youth — Employment — England — Case studies.
I. Title. II. Series: English working class.
III. Series: Christian social union handbooks.
HN398.N49R87   1980   942   79-56944
ISBN 0-8240-0123-0

Printed in the United States of America

A GARLAND SERIES

THE ENGLISH
WORKING CLASS

A Collection of
Thirty Important Titles
That Document and Analyze
Working-Class Life before
the First World War

Edited by
STANDISH MEACHAM
University of Texas

CHRISTIAN SOCIAL UNION HANDBOOKS
Edited by HENRY SCOTT HOLLAND, D.D.

SOCIAL PROBLEMS OF THE NORTH

BY CHARLES E. B. RUSSELL, M.A.

I have been assisted throughout these Hand-books, in all the work that falls to an Editor, by the advice and judgment of Dr. Rashdall, to whom the Executive had authorised me to turn for help, and who has always given me all that I asked for.

HENRY SCOTT HOLLAND.

CHRISTIAN SOCIAL UNION HANDBOOKS
Edited by HENRY SCOTT HOLLAND, D.D.

SOCIAL PROBLEMS

OF THE NORTH

BY

CHARLES E. B. RUSSELL, M.A.

AUTHOR OF 'MANCHESTER BOYS,' 'WORKING LADS' CLUBS,'
'YOUNG GAOL-BIRDS,' ETC.

A. R. MOWBRAY AND CO., Ltd.
LONDON: 28 MARGARET ST., OXFORD CIRCUS, W.
OXFORD: 9 HIGH STREET

PREFACE

In the preparation of this little volume for publication, I have been particularly indebted to Mr. T. C. Horsfall of Macclesfield, one of the foremost social reformers of our day, for the care with which he has gone through the MS., and for the many suggestions which he has made.

I also wish to acknowledge the help I have received from Mr. F. G. D'Aeth and Mr. F. J. Marquis of Liverpool, Mr. Alfred Whitley of Halifax, Miss Blair, the Rev. J. Lightfoot, and Mr. S. P. Grundy of Manchester, Miss S. Reddish of Bolton, Dr. H. Scurfield of Sheffield, and in particular from Mr. H. B. Saint of Newcastle, among many others.

CHARLES E. B. RUSSELL.

Manchester, *September* 1913.

NOTE

BISHOP WESTCOTT, the first President of the Christian Social Union, predicted that as the nineteenth century had been a century of advance in physical science, so the twentieth century would be one of social progress. His prophecy seems to be finding fulfilment. Beyond all doubt there is social movement. Whether the movement will bring progress depends on the ideals which inspire the moving forces. The purpose of the Christian Social Union is to do all that lies in its power to keep Christian ideals to the front. It desires to present Christ as the living Master and King, the enemy of wrong and selfishness, the power of righteousness and love. On the one hand, it holds that ' all social reforms will be vain that are not rooted in a religious creed, a definite faith in God and in human nature, and definite duties of Church membership.' [1] On the other hand, it believes that ' every amelioration of the outward conditions of man's life is the translation of a fragment of our creed into action.' [2]

First, the Christian Social Union seeks to stir

[1] Gore, Sermon on ' The Peril of Drifting.'
[2] Westcott, *The Incarnation—a Revelation of Human Duties.*

up the conscience of Churchmen to the urgency of social problems, and to the Christian duty of working for their solution. That task is certainly not completed. Next, it seeks to substitute for futile sentimentalism that real knowledge of the facts which can only come from hard study. Finally, it encourages its members, often in co-operation with other agencies, to take part in practical efforts at social amelioration, not as bungling amateurs, but as trained workers who know their business.

The experience of the Union has been that it is possible to unite Church people of very different schools of religious and political thought in this effort at applied Christianity. The object of these handbooks is to arouse interest in various social questions, to provide sound information, and to stimulate to further study and to more effective action. The books are the work of specialists in the several subjects. The Christian Social Union does not hold itself corporately responsible for every statement which the handbooks may contain, but it supports the writers with cordial and grateful goodwill in their effort to further the principles of the Union, and it commends their work to all who believe that the Sovereignty of Christ should extend over every part of human life.

J. A. LICHFIELD,
President of C.S.U.

CONTENTS

CHAPTER I

THE FIELD

In the following pages an endeavour is made to sketch certain aspects of the life of the workers of the North of England, more particularly of those who dwell in its great manufacturing centres. There need be no apology for the attempt. Most of the books written in this country on such subjects deal exclusively with London, with but a few noteworthy exceptions such as Mr. Rowntree's *Poverty* and Lady Bell's *At the Works*. In other parts of the country there seems to be a tendency to forget that the North has its difficulties and its claims no less than has London. And whether in North or South few hear the insistent call upon all who can in any way further the interests of their less fortunate fellows to come forward and strive to improve conditions, largely the result of the peculiar economic features of the age, which are inimical to the best interests of the people.

The truth is that the magnitude and importance to the whole country of the social problems of the North have never been sufficiently grasped because people have not realised the vastness of the population concerned. London with its five million inhabitants has made effective appeal to the imagination of the philanthropic, but it has never been brought home to them that an even larger and in parts more crowded population may be found elsewhere. Within the districts covered by Manchester and Liverpool with the contiguous towns there teems a population of over seven millions, and however great the destitution and misery which certain parts of London may present, it is doubtful whether the degradation in its meanest streets in any way equals the degradation of the lowest classes in Liverpool. During the railway strike of 1911 there arose from the depths of that city a people so savage and so degenerate as to horrify witnesses of the riots that took place, compelling many even of the most thoughtless to reflect on what must be the future of a nation which could show such a population, and on what were the causes which led to its existence. The only possible conclusion was that there must be something wrong with the social and economic conditions, something which required altering if future years were not to have greater disaster in store. And Liverpool, with its population of 748,000, does not stand alone, for from the heart of Manchester and Salford with their 948,000, Leeds with its 446,000, and Newcastle with its 267,000, in great moments of popular excitement and periods of industrial strife not altogether dissimilar crowds might pour forth—crowds bereft of self-respect and of all that represents healthy and virile manhood, and still more bereft of that decent, dignified womanhood which one would like to think characteristic of our land. All these cities, mainly industrial in population, are far too densely inhabited at the centre, and terribly lacking in arrangements for public cleanliness, smoke-prevention, and air-space. In none of them has any general care for the people been developed as the prosperity of the districts has advanced. In each much of what is seen to-day is the result of the extraordinary advance in mechanical invention, and the rapid displacement of muscle by machinery during the past century. The tendency has been for great works and factories to multiply in close proximity one to the other, and for masters to require an ever-increasing number of men, whilst few have thought of the conditions under which their employees would live when working hours were over. The men, due at work at an early hour in the morning, have of necessity endeavoured to reside as close as possible to their employment.

The result of all this has been gross overcrowding in central areas, with an inevitable consequent decline in the general morality of the people. In the course of time many of the more highly paid workmen, able to afford tram or railway fares, have moved from the centre of the city; but for the more humble no such migration has been possible, so that the most crowded and central areas are usually occupied by the poorly paid and casual labourers with little wholesome leaven of the more well-to-do amongst them. Rents are extortionately high, yet many of the habitations are totally unfit for healthy life; the streets are dark and ill-paved; and it is small wonder that the trend of modern industrial life has been to lead to an enormous increase—an increase which is only now beginning to be checked—in drunkenness, vicious living, and the prevalence, no less deplorable in the North than in the South, of the national scourge, phthisis.

The need for improved education is similarly pressing, and ' half-time ' is peculiarly a problem of the North.   On every hand it is felt by those who have the interests of the children at heart that no child should be permitted to lead the double life of factory and school, and that the time has come when the termination of its attendance at an elementary school, frequently at so low an age as thirteen, and even at twelve, should not be for it the end of all instruction, but that some scheme of Trades Schools or compulsory Continuation Schools is necessary.   The medical supervision and physical training of the child are also more and more being recognised as functions of the Education Authorities, the physique of the growing population causing long-belated concern.   Apart from the actual diseases, ailments, and imperfections of an enormous percentage of children a certain supineness or flabbiness, quite distinctly to be marked in the adolescents of the day, demands some means of counteraction.   The importance of such problems cannot be overestimated, for it is precisely these disabilities affecting the working-class youth of both sexes which lie in the background of many of the evils which corrode the nation's life.   Adult unemployment, for example, with the grave phenomenon of the existence of the unemployable, is in itself in many ways the result of the continual drift of young persons to occupations which present no opportunity for a useful adult career, and this drift in turn may find its explanation in a system of education which has aimed at little but the imparting of knowledge, and has loosed its hold on the child so early.   Only now is the nation waking up to the importance of education having a bearing upon the future industrial career of the boy, and only now is an attempt being made to place boys at occupations which seem to correspond to their capabilities.

Though, happily, in most of the large centres of population there are signs of a decrease in excessive drinking, no one at all familiar with the conditions existing in northern slum districts can fail to be aware of the terrible evil wrought by drunkenness. Few who have close acquaintance with the subject would be prepared to deny that the extremes of poverty, dirt and dinginess, drabness and ugliness, overcrowding and stuffiness, combined with the deadly monotony of life, are in themselves the inducement for recourse to alcohol as the only means of relief available in such wretched surroundings. The low public-house is a curse, but there is practically no other place where a man may take refuge from the distractions and discomfort of his infant-ridden home. If habits of drunkenness are the result of frequenting the public-house, the real blame lies very often with a state of society which allows conditions to exist which almost compel men to resort to it. When women take to drink it is most frequently, though not always, the outcome of unutterable misery and servitude in the home.

Surely it should not be impossible, while discouraging the public-house, to set up in its place a substitute which will provide for working-men something of the ordinary amenities of life. Our temperance coffee - palaces — so - called — are frequently cold, cheerless, dirty, and singularly unattractive. It would seem almost as though real good comradeship and jollity were not expected in such places; at any rate they are very often not to be found there. But an example of what might be done in the way of providing alternatives to the public-house has been set at Middlesbrough by the foundation of a pleasant place of resort—a well-warmed, well-lighted hall, 90 feet by 60—where refreshments are supplied at cost prices and music may be heard. Three or four hundred people are admitted daily. The North cannot as yet however show anything to equal the enterprise of the Home Counties Public-House Trust, Ltd., in the South. In Hertfordshire this is said to have ' done more for the promotion of temperance than all the temperance societies together.' Founded less than eleven years ago as the Hertfordshire Public-House Trust Company, it has since extended its business to Essex, Middlesex, Kent, Nottinghamshire, and Sussex, its licensed houses numbering about fifty. Its chief aim is to transform public-houses from mere drinking-shops into clean, comfortable, well-equipped places, where a complete meal may be obtained. Alcoholic drinks are of good quality, but as the manager gets no commission on the sale of these alone of all his commodities, no man is urged to drink. Tea, coffee, or cocoa cost 1d. a cup; cold meat with bread and potatoes, 4d.; bread and cheese and pickles, 2d.; a hot meal, 8d. Tobacco, cigars, and cigarettes may be bought at prices ranging from 1d. upwards, and games and music are provided where possible. Dividends are restricted to five per cent., and although nearly all the public-houses conducted by the Trust were secured owing to the failure of their previous occupants, not only has this amount been paid in full, but a rising margin of profit, amounting in 1913 to over £3000, has been put by. Public-houses run on similarly public-spirited lines would be warmly welcomed in

Lancashire and Yorkshire, and would undoubtedly reduce the consumption of alcohol. The experiment is being tried in Cheshire. But this whole question of drinking forms a problem which can only be solved, I believe, by the large-hearted devotion of men and women of all creeds to the service of humanity, and that expressed not only in the personal endeavour to bring something of brightness and worthy experience into the lives of the masses, but by service on the many administrative bodies which at present are often unable to secure the aid of those who, by their wider knowledge and more enlightened views, are best fitted to be their members.

Again, there is the question of the amusements of the people, the use of their leisure hours. At present the commonest custom is to devote spare time entirely to what is light and vapid. The coming of the kinematograph theatre has been in many ways a great boon, but its management caters as a rule only for the less serious tastes of the audience, neglecting the instructive possibilities of photographic films. Meanwhile, what evidence is there of the contemplation and study of Nature, of enjoyment of Art in its various forms, of delight in reading books? All such pleasures, the pleasures of true civilisation, which should appeal no less to the poor man than to the rich, are for lack of opportunity or early training a region entirely unexplored by the majority of the workers. Here, too, it is the advice and direction of those who understand and appreciate these things which is urgently needed. As it is, the pressure of life, and more particularly the 'speeding-up' in connection with all industries, combined with the increasing monotony of the work itself, is resulting in more severe reaction when the day's work is over. This takes the form of a demand for exciting relaxation of one kind or another, a desire which is mainly manifested in the terrible increase of gambling. Gambling is a vice which now certainly vies with drunkenness as the immediate cause of untold calamity in thousands of homes.

No less to be reckoned with, as in the South, so also in the North, is sexual immorality. In some of the cotton towns of Lancashire evidence may be found that the problem is not so predominantly an economic one as many would have us believe, for here, where women's work is more highly paid and more in demand than in any other part of the country, a deplorably low standard of conduct in the relationship of the young people of the opposite sexes is often observable. This canker at the heart of what might be an uncommonly prosperous social life can only, I believe, be successfully combated by the right education of youth, the provision of higher interests, and the inculcation of those ideals of righteousness which must emanate from any true conception of Christianity.

There is also to be considered the growing dissatisfaction of the poor with their condition as compared with that of the very wealthy, whom they are coming to regard as the unheeding parasites of their grinding toil. If it has done nothing else, the education which all now receive has produced in the mind of the worker much clearer conceptions of the relative positions of capital and labour. At the same time there has been a continual widening of the gulf between employer and employed, largely the result of the decay of the private employer and the growth of the soulless limited company, but largely also the result of legislation. As the State gradually assumes more and more the right of dictating the precise relationship between employer and employed, the former is less and less disposed to feel his human responsibilities towards his work-people, being satisfied that he is carrying out the requirements of the law, and that the law has provided in the workman's interests for every eventuality. The invention of the motor-car has proved another severing influence, since it has increased the tendency for the manufacturer or merchant to live far from his business premises and the homes of his employees, so that it is now only in the rarest cases that their families and his are in any way acquainted or endowed with mutual understanding. It is probable that in no northern city is the divergence between classes so marked as it is becoming in Manchester. Among the 80,000 inhabitants, for example, of Hulme, the poorest and most neglected district of the city, is to be found only a tiny minority of persons of much education or refinement, these being with rare exceptions doctors, or ministers of the various religious denominations, and their wives. Moreover, at no time in our history have riches been more ostentatiously displayed and more recklessly squandered. Were the more independent and virile-minded artisans and labourers of the North placed in close contact with the extravagant, vicious folly displayed by wealth in London and the resorts of fashion, in some period of bad trade and consequent suffering, such as was endured with comparative patience and restraint in the winters of 1907 and 1908, there might well occur a violent upheaval of the social order. Happily, riches are not so mercilessly and arrogantly flaunted before the eyes of the northern poor; happily a fair proportion of those who possess them are not without a sense of responsibility and public spirit, and it may be hoped that the inevitable revolution which is taking place in English life will continue its moderate-paced and bloodless course till justice and equity prevail. Meanwhile, although the old sympathy between employer and employed has perhaps died out, something at any rate may be done to bridge the gulf by those who, born to an easy lot, are moved by the disabilities of the humbler worker, and set themselves so far as they can to understand and ameliorate his condition.

Finally, there is the hardest problem of all, the problem of the spiritual life of the people. At bottom the nation is religious, but there can be no doubt that indifference to religion has developed in recent years; possibly as the result of lifeless formalism in some of the Churches; possibly as the outcome of a want of correspondence between Sunday and week-day life in many of their nominal members; possibly, alas, because to superficial observers it has sometimes seemed that the professors of religion are on the side of the rich, and tacitly share their enjoyment of the good things of life without any effort to enter into and appreciate the hardships and cravings of the poor! It is unfortunate that religious bodies in general have not always identified themselves with great movements of social reform, and that in fact in numerous cases it has been left to individuals of all sects to do, without the co-operation of their Churches, the Christ-like work which has been done in every city

for religion and humanity. Thus the Churches
have lost opportunities, and with them the sympathy and confidence of that sincerest of critics,
the working man.[1] Often philanthropists are too
shy of letting their religious motive transpire, and
though the impulse which has moved them to help
their fellows has sprung from the Church, no one
recognises it as one of the fruits by which the Church
may be known. The problem is how to preserve,
restore, and deepen the religious life of the masses.
This much alone is clear—that for its solution is
demanded, as the initial minimum, an active
expression on the part of all good Christians of
their love for their fellow-men. It is certain that no
regeneration, no new life, can be expected to arise
from slum areas without inspiration; and that
inspiration, so far as I can see, must come from
those who have enjoyed advantages in their own
earlier years, and who, having learnt the value of
knowledge, feel that for them it is a duty to impart
what they can of it to their neighbours.

Let it be quite clearly understood that this can
in no way be done by anything which takes the
form of patronage, but only in a spirit of real
brotherhood. Anything short of this may only
spell disaster, as I fear it may have done in many
misdirected efforts of religious persons who have
entered humble homes with all the airs and graces
of superior persons, and left behind them not
softened feelings but increased bitterness.

Apart from this warning, I would not for a

---

[1] How true this is will be admitted by any who have come
in contact with the extraordinary efforts of men of the stamp
of the late Canon Barnett, or Father Dolling, and compare the
feeling in the districts specially influenced by them with that
in any of the less fortunate of our industrial parishes.

moment dictate the direction which work undertaken from a religious motive and for a religious
end should take, for it is a truism that there are
countless paths by which man may be led to God.
For example, apart from any comprehensive housing scheme, much may be done to brighten and
ultimately spiritualise the life of the dweller in poor
artisan districts, not only by means of university
and other settlements, but by the deliberate efforts
of individuals who will set to work to organise
concerts, clubs, and opportunities for people of
both sexes to meet in pleasant companionship.
Among the younger people the field for work of all
kinds is practically limitless.   It is true that various
organisations having for their object the welfare
and training of boys in particular are doing an
immense amount of really valuable work, but
thousands still remain unaffected. The need for
more work among girls is even greater.

Many who have not the particular qualifications
for gaining the affection of the worker yet possess
gifts which might be employed very usefully upon
various administrative bodies, as I have already
suggested in connection with the drink problem.
It is obvious that our Town Councils, Boards of
Guardians, Education Committees, and others are
greatly in need of educated and enlightened men
and women, persons whose horizon is not bounded
by any narrow conceptions of civic advantage, who
are not always and for ever considering the rates
and not the people ; persons who will administer for
to-morrow and not only for to-day.

If, therefore, there is one appeal more than
another I would venture to make, it is this.   That
those who have had the good fortune to be educated

at our public schools and at our universities, who
have been born and bred in the North, and whose
parents have drawn from the labours of the people
of the North the wealth which has enabled them so
to benefit their children, should hear the call of the
North; and, feeling the demand of their own home
centres to be for them far more insistent than the
demand even of the great Metropolis, should throw
themselves into the social work of Leeds, Liverpool,
Manchester, Newcastle, or wherever they may
happen to be placed.

It is mainly with the hope of interesting a few
such men and women that these pages are written.

CHAPTER II

THE APATHY OF THE PEOPLE

ALTHOUGH the statement may be startling to some, there are few experienced in any kind of social work who will not agree that one of the greatest, if not the greatest, of all the difficulties that have to be overcome is the surprising indifference of the people most concerned towards the circumstances in which they find themselves. The lower they are in the social scale, the more in need of changed conditions, the more hopelessly apathetic they become, until in the deepest slough of wretchedness nothing will induce them to stir on their own behalf.

It is true that at odd moments the most unfortunate and reckless of the population are stirred to action, but when this happens it is only the outcome apparently of something that appeals directly to their narrow class interests. Unhealthy habitations may be endured, an epidemic of disease may sweep the district, wages may be reduced to an absolute minimum, and yet no sign of any movement is made. But let there suddenly arise in the heart of a community a strike or economic disturbance—some event that gives scope for hatred—and suddenly from the back streets of city or town there pours out a horde of ragged, dirty, degraded-looking beings, whose one and only object appears to be pillage and the overthrow of whatever forces of law and order may be arrayed against them.

In no way perhaps is the apathy of the people in general more marked than in the state of patient endurance, or possibly it would be truer to say of passive resentment and sullen hopelessness, in which whole families live under entirely unhealthy conditions without any protest to the landlord or the local authority. It is an unhappy commentary on the boasted independence of the Englishman that it is entirely exceptional for any improvement in housing conditions to have been effected by the pressure of the people themselves. They simply will not co-operate in, much less initiate, any efforts for bettering these matters ; on the contrary they are rather inclined to view all changes with suspicion, and to fear that in some way or other the cost of what is done will in the end come home to them.[1] If a man is out of work he will probably never think of applying at the nearest Labour Exchange, and rarely look at the columns of a newspaper to see where workmen such as he are wanted. He will be content aimlessly to wander round *thinking* he is looking for work, and more actively begging for material help from his neighbours and from any philanthropic agencies in his own district of which he may have heard. The social worker will find himself up against this miserable spirit of flabbiness and helpless indifference wherever he turns, and until he has gained experience will find it hard in face of it to resist impatience and dis-

[1] As a matter of personal experience I may say that during a whole year in which I represented a very poor ward in the Manchester City Council I never received a single complaint from a constituent.

couragement. The young enthusiast, for example, who imagines that the crowd will be willing to listen to a course of lectures, however attractive and however useful, is doomed to find his enthusiasm damped by the paucity of the attendances, and even he or she who would bring down into the lowest courts and alleys something of the joy and delight of inspiring music will probably be received at first with anything but enthusiasm. Clubs, unless they are drinking-clubs—and then they are frequently worse than any public-house—do not seem to attract in any large measure the denizens of slum areas ; temperance billiard-halls are only for the few, and those the comparatively well-off; church and chapel institutions have a tendency to become exclusive and ' superior.' Even the possession of the franchise and the excitement of an election stir in no way the heart of the casual labourer, who, when urged to express his political opinions through the ballot-box, will frequently decline with an expression of the sentiment: ' It don't matter to me who gets in. They 're all for theirsels whoever wins.' If appeal is made to the man's patriotic feelings, he may quite possibly answer that it does not matter to him whether a foreign power or our own king rules the country so long as he gets his wages. Marked as it is in the men, the same apathy is no less characteristic of the women, and small wonder in view of the unrelieved drabness, ill-health, toil, and weariness of their lives. The very boys and girls are infected with it, and often even abstain from participation in pleasures whose pursuit involves a little trouble in the way of regularity, punctuality, or perseverance. Almost the greatest need of our time, in fact, is that of breaking through this icy surface of indifference which freezes all the mental powers, and largely accounts for many of the worst features of the slums of the North. But it is impossible to force a higher standard of life upon the people. They must be led to form it for themselves.

If we try to discover from what causes this apathy arises, of exactly what evil conditions it is the effect, we shall have no difficulty in reaching a diagnosis, and since correct appreciation of a disease is the first step towards its cure, we at least have no excuse for pessimism. Any student of the subject must very quickly discover that at the bottom lies the fact that the apathy of the lower working-classes is attributable to two causes, namely, poverty, with its chronic partial starvation or malnutrition, and class distinction.

The casual labourer knows that in the labour market to-day his best efforts from early morning till late at night may result in his earning at the outside 22s. or 23s. a week, and at the lowest a bare 18s. He married perhaps as a young fellow in his early twenties, earning about the same wages, heedless of the future and all it had in store, and failing altogether to calculate what the cost of his subsequent young family would mean. His wife has been able to work but little in the intervals between child-bearing, and now with the care of four or five little ones is totally unable to add anything to the family income. The man sees before him a vista of years in which his earnings will never be more. He knows his wife and children, like himself, are not being fed as they should be fed. He cannot even provide for them the coveted Sunday clothes, the hall-mark of respectability, without which the family must perforce sink into a lower stratum of society. The well-dressed avoid his quarters, and the Christian fellowship of which he has heard so much in his young days means to him nothing. In fact he often finds more charity, generosity, kindly feeling, and forgiveness for his shortcomings in neighbours who make no claim at all to Christianity. In the background of his life lies that grim terror, the 'House,' always waiting there ready to engulf him and his if ill befall.

He feels that if only he were able to earn a few more shillings a week much might be changed, but that without them it is useless to struggle or to take an interest in anything. If he began by caring, he has had so constantly to forgo and renounce that he has schooled himself to think that nothing is worth while, and rather to pride himself on not being one to make a fuss. In the life-history of man after man may be traced to some such process a gradually growing liking for the public-house and an increasing interest in various forms of gambling, balanced by a decreasing interest in home and family. As a result, in many cases the whole conditions become worse and worse until they resolve themselves into the mere existence of a human unit without hope or ideals of any kind, unless it be the expectation of winning some bet to be spent not upon the household, but in a public-house carouse.

Further, the more men of this class realise the difficulty of finding fresh employment, the more hopelessly do they feel themselves under the thumb of their employers. For, never having learnt to save even a few pence, such men have never learnt to organise themselves so as to obtain better economic conditions. The casual labourer dare not struggle alone, for he would be discharged. He does not trust his fellows, and hesitates to hand over to any society a portion of his earnings as a fee for combination. So he remains the apathetic and indifferent, unhappy-looking creature too painfully well known to every observer.

I have said his condition is the result of poverty and of class distinction, and it may be argued that so far as the poverty is concerned ultimately legislation alone can bring relief. This is so to a large extent, yet there is no question but that even under present economic conditions much of all this pitiful waste of human potentialities might be avoided were not gold so great a god. In the pursuit of riches the humbler agents through whom riches are obtained become entirely forgotten, and duty toward one's neighbour is too often translated into the smallest silver coin of the realm placed with some reluctance in the offertory plate at the Sunday collection ' for the poor.' [1] If Christianity be not to-day the living faith which one would have it be throughout the land, the failure must be laid to the fact that Money, not God, has become the motive-power in the lives of so many who believe they are Christians.

With regard to class distinction—and by class distinction I do not mean merely the broad division into rich and poor, but include also all those *nuances* of caste which are so pitilessly observed among the middle and working-classes—the problem should be a somewhat simpler one. What has been

[1] A recent Sunday morning collection at a church whose congregation is one of the wealthiest in the country contained no fewer than one hundred and twenty threepenny-bits.

achieved in various cities in connection with many
settlements and missions is a proof, if proof were
needed, that real kindly interest, real friendship,
and real sympathy may and do break through the
icy apathy I have described. Men and women of
education and high ideals, who voluntarily live with
and for the poor, whether as individuals or communities, may pervade a whole district with broader
views of humanity, and substitute ties of fellowship
for petty social barriers.   Imperceptibly perhaps,
but surely, apathy is thawed in the process, and
new life and hope spring up even amid the winter
of poverty.

I have entitled this chapter ' The Apathy of the
People,' but it is almost with shame I must acknowledge that my theme has been only the apathy of
the poor.   What of the apathy of the well-to-do ?
How dare we, to whom birth and education have
given eyes to see, go through our streets and behold
the sights that are to be seen there—the tattered
child, bare-footed, pinched in feature, covered with
sores, and dirt, and vermin ; the baby crawling
in the filth of the back-street gutter ; the woman,
ragged, unkempt, slatternly, unwashed, careless of
appearance, every inch of her body coarsened and
degraded ; the corner-loafer, vile of countenance,
obscene of language ; the streets themselves, ill-
cleaned, disfigured with garbage ; the houses, mean
and grimy, showing no sign of such seemliness or
beauty as becomes habitations for self-respecting
human beings ; the very air polluted with offensive,
germ-laden dust in summer, and with sooty fog
in winter—how dare we, who see these things and
yet from day to day go about our business in silence,
tolerating them—how dare *we* criticise the apathy

of the poor ? More than ten years ago a foreign visitor to London recorded his impressions in the following words, which he might equally well have applied to almost any city of the North :

> ‘ The first impressions received by one who passes through the working-class districts in London are so disgusting that most visitors are deterred from ever paying a second visit. One can go miles without seeing a dress or a shoe which is in good condition. This neglect of dress is found in people of both sexes and of all ages. Then there is the monotony of the rows of houses, the filthiness of the streets, and, more than all else, the fact that here and there the eye falls on a member of that wretched army of so-called “ street-arabs,” who are about the most horrifying human beings that the eye of a continental doctor can meet with. . . . These and similar impressions, deepened by the sight of drunken men and women whom one occasionally sees lying in the side streets, prevail when one first visits the London workmen’s districts. . . . *The indifference with which high and low pass these unhappy, almost bestial, but free-born Britons is well-nigh incomprehensible to a foreigner.*’ [1]

Other continental critics have used equally forcible language, but we are no more stung to action by the shame of so deep a reproach than by the facts themselves.

The poor are indifferent, apathetic. Poverty is their excuse. What is ours ?

[1] Dr. A. Grotjahn in Weyl's *Handbuch der Hygiene*, 1902. The italics are mine.

CHAPTER III

INFANCY

MUCH as I should like to shirk a subject on which I feel only women and medical men are fully qualified to write, it seems impossible to undertake a general survey of social conditions without referring to matters of such primary importance as are motherhood and infancy. Nobody will deny that if we could secure the birth of none but healthy children, and their upbringing by healthy, happy, good mothers to the age when they go to school, the magnitude of the problems of later life would be diminished by at least a half, and the nation would be enormously stronger and richer. The amount of human material wasted in infant mortality is appalling to contemplate, and not less appalling is the fact that the wretched lives of the greater proportion of the degenerates who fill our prisons, workhouses, asylums, hospitals, and institutions of every kind have been predetermined from infancy, from birth, even from conception.[1] If the degree of civilisation is to be estimated by the value placed

---

[1] ' The dead baby is next of kin to the diseased baby, who in time becomes the anæmic, ill-fed, and educationally backward child, from whom is derived, later in life, the unskilled " casual," who is at the bottom of so many of our problems.'—Dr. A. K. Chalmers, quoted in the *Minority Report of the Poor Law Commission,* 1909.

on human life—and this, I believe, is the usual
criterion—what are we to think of our condition as
a nation ?   Substitute for the term ' human life '
the life of horses, oxen, sheep, or pigs, and we might
have some occasion for pride, for it has been truly
said that no farmer would tolerate such mortality
among his young stock as we tolerate among our
infants.   Every year now in this country some
ninety thousand babies perish before reaching twelve
months of age,[1] and it would probably be a low
estimate to regard sixty thousand of these deaths
as preventible.   Is there not a certain irony about
the chivalry which in case of sudden danger—a railway accident or shipwreck, for example—always
cries, ' Save the women and children ! '   Men are
willing to give their lives in a moment of peril; at
other times they ignore the fact that women are
suffering and children are dying unheeded and un-
helped for want, not of the sacrifice of other lives,
but only of thought and care.

This is peculiarly a problem of the North.   Taking
the whole of the United Kingdom, it is upon Lancashire that the heaviest burden of shame rests, and
a list of the six next worst counties comprises
Northumberland, Durham, and the West Riding of
Yorkshire.   Of the twenty-five towns with the
highest rates of infant mortality between 1907 and
1910, ten are in Lancashire and eighteen lie north
of latitude 53.   In the worst town of all, Stalybridge,
the rate was 189.0 per thousand.   Compare this
with Hornsey and Bromley, for example, where the
rates are 66.8 and 68.1 respectively.   Both are
within five miles of the City of London, and even

---

[1] Only some three years ago the number was estimated at
120,000.

there the infantile death-rate for the same period was no more than 78.0 per thousand.

Bad housing, bad sanitation, dirt, drunkenness, and immorality [1] always lie at the back of a high rate of infant mortality. But undoubtedly the evil pre-eminence of the North in this ghastly slaughter of the innocents is due to an additional cause, namely, the industrial employment of married women, with the resulting want of care for the infant both before and after birth. In Lancashire alone in the textile industry there are more than 300,000 women workers,[2] and in Lancashire and Yorkshire together there are over 130,000 married women in the mills.[3] The most terrible feature of the indictment is that in the main it is *not* a problem of poverty. Many babies' deaths are no doubt due to the starvation and misery of their mothers, but the greater proportion cannot be thus excused. As Mr. Burns remarked at the last Annual Conference of the National Association for the Prevention of Infant Mortality [4] : ' It may be said that where industry prospers, and married women work, there children decay.' In the cotton towns, in homes where £2, £3, £4 a week or more are being earned, and gramophones, pianos, and other luxuries are common, one might imagine that a prospective mother would take every care of herself and her infant. On the contrary, many a one values her

---

[1] The proportion of deaths of illegitimate children is always enormously higher. In 1910 in Manchester the proportion under one year was 125 legitimate and 306 illegitimate. In Salford for the years 1902-11 the death-rate of infants under one year averaged 159 per thousand legitimate and 304 per thousand illegitimate. Disease is one factor.

[2] *The Englishwoman*, June 1910.

[3] *The Millgate Monthly* (Manchester), April 1913.

[4] August 4, 1913, London.

wages so highly that she will work up to the last possible day, and return again to the mill when her baby is but a fortnight old or even less, leaving it to the care of a more or less incompetent neighbour, and all the dangers of artificial feeding. I have it as the deliberate opinion of an observant young man, who himself works in a mill in the north of Lancashire, that the root cause of much infant-neglect is love of money. On Sundays and holidays the woman mill-worker likes to appear exceedingly well dressed. She frequently pays four or five guineas for a costume, and in proportion for other articles of clothing. To give up going to the mill and devote herself to the bearing and rearing of children would entail the abandonment of all this —of her social pleasures. The ignorant victim of false standards, she refuses to make the sacrifice, and prefers to immolate her children, her future health, and the comfort of her home to Mammon.[1]

Of course the evil is by no means at an end with the deaths of children under one year. The death-rate during the next four years of life is proportionately high, in Stalybridge again being 166 on a calculation of a general average of 100.[2] Further, many of the children who survive must, obviously, have ruined constitutions. 'While thousands perish outright, hundreds of thousands who worry through are injured in the hard struggle for exist-

[1] Whilst I make these grave charges, let me not be thought to bring them against all the women mill-workers. Far from it, for in general there is no class of women more deserving of respect, no class in which more sterling qualities can be found. Those who neglect their children are women of the same type as those who neglect their children elsewhere, and are probably not proportionately more numerous. The fact that highly paid work is easily within their reach makes the fatal difference.

[2] *The Manchester Guardian*, August 5, 1913.

ence and grow up weaklings, physical and mental degenerates. *A high infantile mortality rate, therefore, denotes a far higher infantile deterioration rate.'* [1] And if we turn from the purely physical side of the question, the deprivation of a proper home life must be an incalculable loss. For what is the life of the woman mill-worker ? She rises at 5 or 5.30, takes the child or children out to be nursed, begins work at 6 A.M., and continues until 12.30, with a break from 8 to 8.30. After preparing and eating dinner she sees the elder children off to school, and then begins work again at 1.30. This goes on till 5.30 P.M., when she returns to take up her home duties—to clean the house, mend and darn, bake and wash. Truly a pitiful life for a mother, and one can but wonder that anything but bare necessity can induce a woman to consent to it. [2]

Legislation such as the Midwives Act and Insurance Act will no doubt have an influence on the rate of infant mortality ; improved housing and sanitation, and the better regulation of women's work, will have still more. But what is needed most of all is a change of heart in many of the mothers. They need to be taught that they are guilty when their babies die, taught to regard such deaths not as the normal visitation of God but extraordinary,

---

[1] *Minority Report of the Poor Law Commission.*

[2] It is distressing to reflect how slowly we progress towards civilisation in matters of this kind. The criticisms of one of Mrs. Gaskell's characters read as freshly as ever after sixty-five years : ' " They oughtn't to go out after they 're married, that I 'm very clear about. I could reckon up " (counting with her fingers), " ay, nine men I know, as has been driven to th' public-house by having wives as worked in factories ; good folk, too, as though there was no harm in putting their little ones out at nurse, and letting their house all go dirty, and their fires all out ; and that was a place as was tempting for a husband to stay in, was it ? He soon finds out gin-shops." '—*Mary Barton,* chapter x.

taught the iniquity of that spreading crime the destruction of incipient life,[1] taught how to feed and wash and tend infants in sickness and in health. Alderman Broadbent, ex-Mayor of Huddersfield, by a famous experiment has shown all England what *can* be done by teaching. Beginning with Longwood, one of the wards of the borough, a place with an infant mortality of 122 per thousand in spite of little work by married women, he offered to pay £1 on the first anniversary of its birth to each baby born between November 9, 1904 and November 9, 1905. Cards giving good advice as to the upbringing of infants were distributed by a committee of ladies, who also paid periodical visits to mothers. As a result the number of deaths for that year was less than half that of preceding years. Later a complete scheme for reducing the mortality in Huddersfield was framed by Alderman Broadbent and Dr. Moore, the Medical Officer of Health, ' of which the *mot d'ordre* is "Help the mother to nurse her infant herself in her own home." ' The result of the first thirty-nine weeks' working (1907) was that the infant mortality figures, which for the corresponding period of the previous year had been 138 per thousand, were reduced to 85. The cost of the work in this first year was at a rate of less than £400 a year, for already a voluntary association of nearly a hundred ladies was helping the two Lady Assistant Medical Officers of Health.

[1] Lady Bell, in *At the Works* (Middlesbrough), chapter viii., brings another severe charge against the women : ' We must remember that the number of children who die is, in some cases, at any rate, due to the fact that the child's life has been insured ; for many a time the parent is acutely conscious that it lessens the burden of life on the whole, that instead of there being another child to look after, its place should be empty and some additional funds come in to compensate for its loss.'

Within the last six years, especially within the last two, an increasing interest in the welfare of infants has found expression in the establishment of so-called ' Schools for Mothers ' and ' Infant Consultation Centres.'   In at least twenty-five northern towns and cities these arrangements have been made for weighing and examining babies, and giving advice and definite teaching to their mothers.   In Bradford, Scarborough, and Sheffield the Public Health Authorities, represented by enthusiastic Medical Officers, have themselves organised such work. The ' City of Bradford Infant Consultations ' is probably the finest organisation of the kind in existence, and provides an example which will, it is to be hoped, be followed by every municipality in the country.   The speed with which its help has been appreciated by the women concerned is indeed phenomenal, seeing that after only eighteen months of existence (to December 1913) it has upwards of 2300 babies on its books, and a weekly average attendance of from 500 to 600, nearly 24,000 ' consultations ' having been held.   An endeavour is made to maintain skilled medical supervision over all working-class infants from birth to the age of two, whilst the education of the mothers by individual, not by class, teaching is a marked feature of the work.   Proper food is supplied for infants who could not otherwise obtain it, and woollen garments are retailed at cost price.   The records kept of every infant in attendance ' are expected to furnish information and statistics of both professional and sociological value on many questions in the field of infant life.'   Not only are the weights and measurements of a baby recorded, but particulars about its family—what its father does, what its mother did before marriage, and whether she still works, how the older children have been fed in infancy, etc.—are noted on cards, which are filed for reference. The staff, which at the start in June 1912 consisted of one lady-doctor and two assistants, by the end of 1913 consisted of two lady-doctors, five nurses, a dispenser, two attendants, and a clerk. A temporary hospital was already provided last summer, and new premises,[1] specially built at a cost of £13,000, comprise a Hospital as well as an Infant Clinic, Milk Modifying Laboratory, Milk Depot, and every department and appliance likely to be useful for the healthful preservation of infant life.[2]

In Sheffield five half-days a week are devoted to similar work, and more than two hundred mothers attend every week, about a thousand receiving expert advice in the course of a year. A doctor paid by the Corporation and two lady-doctors conduct the consultations, and a woman inspector with seventeen assistants (at a salary of from £70 to £104 per annum and uniform), all qualified as nurses and midwives, visit the homes and assist generally in the work. Excellent pamphlets of advice are distributed. Further, a Motherhood League, started in 1907, co-operates with the municipal work, and endeavours to promote the welfare of all children by raising the ideal of home life and educating the mothers by means of entertainments, competitions, lectures, etc. It is encouraging to note that practically all the mothers addressed at meetings were in favour of having

---

[1] To be opened early in 1914.
[2] For further information see *The World's Work*, November 1913.

the leaving age for school girls raised from thirteen
to fourteen, provided that during the last year
they were taught useful subjects such as cookery.
Resolutions to this effect were sent to the Education Committee.[1]   The rate of infant mortality in
Sheffield declined from 200 per thousand in 1900 to
119 in 1909.

Oldham has six Schools for Mothers, Manchester
four branches of one society, and a Roman Catholic
School.   Newcastle a society with two branches
which claims to have contributed to the reduction
of the death-rate from 139 in 1908, its first year of
work, to 101 in 1912 ; Leeds [2] a ' Babies' Welcome '
with six centres; Hull, Bolton, and other towns
flourishing institutions with rapidly increasing
responsibilities.   Burnley, notorious for its high
rate of infant mortality, started similar work with
municipal assistance in February 1912, and is
about to open a second centre, and Stalybridge also
has just established a School for Mothers.   The
Health Committee of the Ashton Town Council
has lately resolved to follow their example in a
ward in which the infantile death-rate is abnormally
high.   ' For eleven months the rate was equal to
159 per thousand, but during November it was
treble that figure.' [3]

The expansion of ' Infant Consultations ' to
include all children under school age, or the provision of ' Inspection Centres ' or ' Nursery Schools,'
possibly as departments of Schools for Mothers, as

[1] *The Child*, March 1913.
[2] The schools in Leeds, Manchester, and Salford earn grants
from the Board of Education for class instruction in cookery,
hygiene, sewing, and knitting.
[3] *The Manchester Guardian*, December 11, 1913.

is recommended by Sir George Newman,[1] would
be of inestimable benefit in securing the medical
supervision of children, and would surely prove a
huge economy to the State.   To quote his Report :

> ' The School for Mothers, with a branch
> Treatment Clinic, and possibly with a Day
> Nursery or Nursery School, carried on largely
> by voluntary effort, but aided and supervised
> by the Central and Local Authority, would
> secure in the district served an opportunity of
> education and training for the mothers, to-
> gether with the continuous supervision of the
> children from birth to school age, and facilities
> for the immediate treatment of the small
> childish ailments which are now so often neg-
> lected and become serious mainly on account
> of this neglect.   Such an organisation offers
> one solution of the problem, now becoming
> more apparent and urgent, as to how provision
> should be made for the effective control and
> care of children below school age without
> taking them unnecessarily from their homes,
> or interfering unduly with the responsibility
> of their parents.'

It is to such efforts, in conjunction with improve-
ments in hygienic and sanitary conditions, that we
must look, not alone for a continued reduction
in the rate of infant mortality, but for the passing
into the elementary schools of healthier, stronger
children.   Seeing what has been accomplished in
five years, it is not too much to hope that ere many
more have elapsed every city district, every town,

---

[1] *Annual Report for* 1912 *of the Chief Medical Officer of the
Board of Education.*

and every village will have its School for Mothers. Thousands of volunteers are required, but if the eyes of our educated young women were but opened to the appalling facts, no doubt they would come forward in adequate numbers to be trained for such work. If they can do nothing else for this cause, let men at least make it their business to bring so vital a matter to the knowledge of their sisters, wives, and mothers.

I cannot close this chapter without referring to the infant mortality for which the Poor Law authorities are directly responsible. The Report of the Poor Law Commission (1909) revealed that in many workhouses a scandalous condition of affairs obtained, and there is little reason, alas, to suppose that there has been a very sweeping improvement during the last four years. It was discovered that the mortality among infants in the Poor Law institutions, where the ordinary dangers from starvation, exposure, and ignorance are presumably absent, was *between two and three times as great* as in the population as a whole, 40 to 45 per thousand dying within a week of birth, and 268 to 392 by the end of the year, 'the number varying according to whether we take the experience of the Poor Law institutions for legitimates or for illegitimates, in the Metropolis, or elsewhere.' In ten workhouses the death-rate was found to be as high as thirty-three per cent. It is a common thing for the children under five years to be entrusted to the care of feeble-minded, aged, and infirm paupers, and in large establishments it is not uncommon for those too young to walk never to be taken into the open air, but to spend the whole period of their residence in the same mephitic atmosphere. In 1897 it was forbidden to employ pauper nurses in workhouse infirmaries. Are the little children of less value than the sick that no similar protective edict has been issued on their behalf ? Clearly what is wanted in our workhouses is an adequate provision of trained *children's* nurses.[1]

I believe it is still rare for expectant mothers in the maternity wards to receive any instruction or expert advice whatever, or to be allowed to occupy the time of waiting by making clothes for the coming infant.

A Lancashire lady writes me that the cruel policy by which respectable widows with infants are by many Boards of Guardians refused out-relief and forced into the workhouse is in itself obviously responsible for the death or ruin of many young children. Unless a home is thoroughly bad, it is always a better place for a child than an institution, and it would be far more economical and far more satisfactory if mothers could be paid to nurse their children in their own homes. Many decent widows could easily keep their homes together if they were paid as much as, or even less than, the Guardians pay other women for taking care of their children when 'boarded out.' Again, when out-relief is granted in maternity cases, it is frequently too

[1] Since I wrote the above paragraph the Local Government Board has issued (December 31) new Orders for the management of Poor Law institutions, which will happily make much of my criticism obsolete. It is provided that every child under eighteen months of age shall be medically examined at least once a fortnight, and those over eighteen months at least every month. Children over three years of age are to be altogether excluded from the workhouses after April 1, 1915. Pauper inmates are no longer to be employed in any capacity in the nurseries, unless approved by the Medical Officer for the particular employment, and acting under the immediate supervision of a paid officer. The Orders are to become effective on April 1, 1914.

meagre, and granted only for a fortnight after the child's birth, so that a working mother may be faced with the alternative of putting the baby out to nurse and resuming her toil, or starving. Only a few months ago this lady came across a fragile-looking young widow, who supported herself and children by trudging twelve or fifteen miles a day with a barrow-load of plants. This she did from the time of the illness and death of her husband right up to the birth of her fourth child five months later. Out-relief, and that not sufficient to cover rent, was granted for a fortnight only, and by the twelfth day she had made plans to hand the baby over to a neighbour, and trudge forth on her weary round of hawking. The one-roomed home was clean, the baby healthy, but the decree of the Guardians might well have proved a sentence of death for both mother and infant.[1]

Until our legislators, our local authorities, our educated classes in general recognise motherhood as a noble and patriotic calling, how shall the poor, pitiable women, the best years of whose lives are

---

[1] The tragedy of a widow's baby was reported in the London papers of November 11, 1913, as follows : ' An inquest was held at Clerkenwell yesterday on Elizabeth M——, aged three months, daughter of a widow of S—— Street, who died from exhaustion. Dr. B—— said the case was a sad one. The mother was engaged as a cleaner-up at a coffee-house, and had to go out to work at 7 A.M. until 8 P.M. She received eight shillings a week, out of which she had to pay two shillings to an aged woman to mind the child and half a crown a week rent. How she managed to keep herself, the infant, and another child was a mystery. There was no doubt that the autumn diarrhœa, from which the baby suffered, was due to improper feeding. This disease caused a large infantile mortality, which would not be remedied until the authorities had solved the housing problem, and made the lives of the poorest more humane. The jury returned a verdict according to the medical evidence.' Such cases are, I fear, only too common.

wasted in a weary round of expecting, bearing, and burying under-valued children, realise their high responsibilities or find help in their woe ? It is not alone a legendary age that requires the chivalrous courage of a Perseus. Poverty, ignorance, indifference—these are the dragons in whose power are bound to their rock of misery the Mothers of the Nation, and a nobler task and higher satisfaction than that of the son of Danaë awaits the slayers of the hydra-headed monsters.

CHAPTER IV

EDUCATION

It is no part of my purpose to devote much space to the consideration of elementary school problems. I am not qualified for such a task, and the scope of this work forbids it. At the same time it is impossible to refrain from noting certain wide aspects of education, for, seeing that perfect education would be the solution of most of our social problems, it should be a subject of vital interest to every one of us, and not alone to the educationist and pedagogue. How it is regarded in the representative assembly of the nation may be indicated by the following passage from a daily newspaper:

' When he [Mr. Pease] rose to make the statement of the year as to how England stands educationally, there was a scurry towards the lobby ; men stood not upon the order of their going, but went at once. The Treasury Bench was empty, save for under-secretaries. Other benches were empty. The House in dreariness was a reflex of atmospheric conditions outside.' [1]

I am hardly likely to count among my readers many of those old-fashioned, reactionary, somewhat stupid persons who go about the world complaining that ' our children are over-educated, and that's what's the matter with them ; for their

[1] *The Standard*, April 11, 1913.

brains are stuffed with a lot of nonsense that's no
earthly good to them, and only makes them think
a deal too much of themselves.' A modern Socrates
would, I think, have no difficulty in convincing
such critics that what is wrong—for there is something wrong, and so far their criticism is justified—is
not that the children are *over*-educated, but that they
are not sufficiently *well*-educated. There has been a
wonderful advance in the art of teaching, and it is
rare now for a child actually to dislike his school.
This is evidenced by the extraordinary decrease in
truancy, except in cases where homes are very bad.
But in spite of the advances that have been made
it is open to question whether the schools to-day
are turning out youths as well fitted for the parts
they will have to play in later life as was the case
when the school curriculum contained far fewer
subjects. No one with any knowledge of the
subject will underestimate the value of the work,
or of the enthusiasm put into it by the teachers,
but they have to carry out schemes and regulations
made for and not by them; and it may often be the
case that the ideas of some official theorist have to
be acted upon rather than the far more practical
and simpler notions of the man who best knows the
needs of the children, whilst the views of persons
who devote themselves to the study of education
can only with difficulty obtain a hearing.

I would not for a moment attempt to suggest a
reformed time-table, but I am convinced that those
Education Committees which during the last few
years have been more or less tentatively introduc-
ing some form of manual training into the curriculum, are on the right track. For I believe that
the fact that so many young people enter what are

called blind-alley occupations, and are rendered unemployable when approaching manhood, is largely attributable to the lack of attention given in many areas to hand work. There can be little doubt that many of those who are turned away from office and shop at eighteen or nineteen years of age, if only they had received good training in early years in the use of simple tools—hammer, chisel, and saw —could be absorbed as handy youths in various profitable callings. And had they been allowed to express themselves in manual work, it is probable that many would possess that power of initiative which is lacking in the average youth of the present time. Many a child, dull and backward at book-learning, would 'find itself' when enabled and required to *make* something, and, saved by the pride and self-respect derived from success in the use of tangible materials, would grow into a bright useful man or woman instead of a 'lame dog.' A well-devised scheme of manual instruction will assign the subject a place of equal importance with the 'Three R's.' It will begin in the infant school, and by the medium of various handicrafts progress throughout the whole school life. Mr. J. G. Legge, Director of Education in Liverpool, has set forth [1] six reasons for the introduction of manual work into elementary schools :

'It was recognised now that manual work of one sort or another was a stimulus to intellectual activity. The development of the brain was largely assisted in the early years of a child's life by a varied and systematic series of physical exercises. Secondly, it was

[1] At a meeting of the Bristol Council of Workers amongst Boys, February 14, 1913.

now a well-ascertained physiological fact that between the ages of seven and fourteen children had a certain dexterity with their fingers which became feebler with every successive year after fourteen. Therefore, if children were to attain to skill in maturity, they must be given the opportunity of exercising their fingers, their wrists, their elbows, and their arms. The third consideration was, they wanted to give scope for the exercise of a child's constructive faculties, or, as there was objection to the word faculties, they might speak of expression through a child's motor activities. The fourth consideration was to make other school subjects more natural to the child, in other words to bring every school subject they possibly could into relation with the third dimension. The fifth was to keep the child in touch with its own environment, to make it realise what life meant to it. Finally, and this was a very important point, and upon it was based the most effective means of character-forming in schools, to give a child something to do which that child recognised was useful. Conditions must be artificial in a school. They could not fail to be, but if they could find anything that was not artificial, not artificial in the child's sense —the moment the child had to make something that was of definite use for itself, it knew it was not working at a mere problem in algebra or mathematics, and was not talking about a country it never had seen or never would see. The moment the child recognised it was dealing with something that was of use to it, and dealing with a condition that was natural to it, the child's interest was invariably aroused, and the child became absorbed in it.'

Though a large proportion of elementary schools now find a place for hand-work in their time-tables, it is often of a very rudimentary nature, and in this matter the majority have something to learn from not a few special and industrial schools. In the best of these very great thought, and care, and expert skill have been devoted to so training children handicapped by physique and environment as to fit them to take their place in the world amongst others who have been more happily circumstanced. It is right that every care and the best possible chance in life should be given to the child rescued from criminal or immoral surroundings, to the little thief, the deaf child, the epileptic, the feeble-minded. But why should the normal children, who are far more numerous and of far greater value to the State, have a less practical education, less well-equipped buildings ? Why ? unless because pity is a commoner virtue than common sense.

The Board of Education pays a special additional grant for manual work taught to children over eleven years of age. It lies therefore rather with the local than with the central Education Authorities to make the next advances.

As an example of what is already being done in this direction by northern Education Committees, I may quote Manchester. In 1911-12, of some 35,000 elementary school children over the age of eleven an average number of 12,613 boys were receiving instruction from 51 teachers in handicraft and light woodwork, and 8089 girls were learning cookery, 3585 laundry, 572 housewifery, whilst 5797, in 81 schools, were instructed in the feeding and tending of infants. With the exception of the last subject most of the teaching was given in centres. The difficulty of giving efficient instruction in such subjects in the ordinary schoolroom is obvious, and it is to be hoped that no plans for new schools will be passed by Education Committees unless they make adequate provision for well-equipped manual-training rooms.

Were it possible at some future date, it would be very desirable that girls also should be taught the use of simple tools, and that boys should learn to mend their own boots and clothing, and to cook plain food. Such knowledge would not only be useful to emigrants, but would also contribute very much to the comfort and economy of many a home, particularly in cases of illness.

There is another subject which I earnestly desire to see taught in some form during the last year of school life. I suppose all who think will admit that one of the most important things in life is sex-relationship, whether we regard the full development and happiness of the individual or the welfare of the nation and race. Yet on this point the school, which is supposed to train a child to live, remains inactive, withholding the knowledge which more than any other knowledge might save and purify. Instruction in sexual hygiene has, I learn, been experimentally given by selected physicians in the higher schools of several German cities, and with such success that the subject is to be, or has already been, introduced into the upper classes of the elementary schools (Volksschulen). I am convinced that if the same plan could be adopted in this country, and plain, but delicately and reverently expressed, teaching as to the nature and functions of their own bodies be given to children during their last year at school by specially qualified persons, incalculably more would be accomplished for the promotion of morality than by all the admirable societies and institutions whose thankless task it is to shut the stable door after the horse is gone. It is pitiful to think of the young lives blighted, destroyed, infecting others with the breath of corruption, simply for want of a little instruction during the critical years when sex-consciousness is aroused. Most of us, I fancy, would blush now to remember certain conversations with schoolfellows and the eagerness with which information, often from most objectionable sources, was received at a time when our natural curiosity was still unsatisfied. Yet we in turn leave our children to rake muck-heaps for the bread of knowledge which should be set before them undefiled.

During the last few years, in many northern schools the encouragement of plant-growing has proved an excellent aid to the training of children in habits of thoughtfulness and care. In some areas, *e.g.* Blackburn, the young plants are distributed free by the Parks Committees, in other cases a charge of a penny or twopence is made, whilst in Leeds the Education Committee has made a grant of £75 per annum for the purchase of plants and seeds. In Manchester, in the autumn of 1911, 152,000 bulbs were applied for by the scholars, and during the following summer 25,000 plants were supplied and 9000 certificates of merit gained by the growers. Gardens have been formed recently at some few city and suburban municipal schools.

Practically all students of education are agreed as to the necessity for raising the school leaving age to at least fourteen without exceptions. At present there is no uniformity, as the regulations vary in different parts of the country. It may be estimated roughly that only a fourth of the children of the country are attending school under regulations which provide that they shall continue in attendance until they have reached fourteen years of age or passed Standard VII. In other areas children may leave at thirteen, and in some cases at so low an age as twelve. In a recent interview [1] Mr Graham, Director of Education in that city, estimated that '90 per cent. of the children who attend elementary schools in Leeds receive no further education at all,' and stated that it is only in exceptional cases that children remain at school beyond the earliest leaving age, which in that area is thirteen. Many of them at once begin to work for sixty hours a week, which largely explains why so few go on to Continuation Schools.

Whatever the leaving age may be, under no authority in England is there any kind of provision for compulsory continued education, and the demand for juvenile labour at the present day being in many districts in excess of the supply, the result is that the vast bulk of the young people of the country are just ceasing their education at the time the public schoolboy is seriously beginning his; and at the time too, when, to quote Mr Graham again, ' the teachers and all connected with education feel that the children are just on the point

[1] *Westminster Gazette*, November 12, 1913.

of gaining some advantage from what has been taught them, and their minds have been prepared just sufficiently to enable them to form judgments for themselves.' This would not be nearly so serious a matter if, on leaving school, they entered callings which were educative. Generally speaking they do not, and at seventeen or eighteen years of age have forgotten most of what they learned at school, can often only write extremely slowly and badly, know little of arithmetic, and read only the evening and comic papers. The obligation to attend school ceasing at so early an age, it is not perhaps surprising that there has been no national scheme for continued education. Education authorities in various parts of the country have realised the need gradually, and schemes differing widely in their scope have been set up to provide the instruction felt necessary. Unfortunately the results have been little commensurate with the efforts put forth, for employers as a class have been greedy for cheap labour, and the average boy quite naturally would rather be a wage-earner than a scholar. But this subject belongs to the next chapter.

What is known as the Half-time System is a curse almost peculiar to Lancashire and Yorkshire. In other counties it is rare except in agricultural labour, in which it is much less harmful. The system originated in 1835, when children under nine years of age were prohibited from working in factories, and the hours for those over that age, but under thirteen, were restricted to forty-eight per week. In 1879 the age was raised to ten, in 1893 to eleven, and finally in 1899 to twelve, full time being allowed after thirteen, if exemption from school

has been granted. The number of children thus
employed went down from 1892, when there were
172,363 half-timers in England and Wales, to 1902;
but, whereas in 1903-4 the number was 78,876, in
1905-6 it was 82,328. The great majority of the
children who work as half-timers are engaged in the
cotton and worsted mills, but some also in miscel-
laneous occupations in the mill districts. The term
' half-timer ' means that they are employed on
alternate days in the mill and in school, or more
frequently that in alternate weeks they spend the
mornings in school and afternoons at work, and
vice versâ. One week they may be in school
twelve and a half hours and in the mill thirty hours,
the next week fifteen hours in school and twenty-
six at work. Morning work commonly lasts from
6 or 6.30 A.M. till 12.30, afternoon work from 1 to
5.30 or 6 P.M., though the children must not work
more than four and a half hours at a stretch, or
more than five and a half in all per day. In a large
proportion of cases these hours have to be spent
in a damp, tropical atmosphere[1] amid a deafen-
ing whir of machinery. ' In the cotton mills of
Lancashire the half-timer is employed either as
"little piecer" or "doffer" in the spinning-room,
piecing together the broken ends of thread, or re-
placing the big bobbins that have become empty;
as "tenter" in the weaving-shed, or "knotter" at
the knotting-bench. In the weaving-shed the
threads, made in the spinning-room, are woven by
looms into cloth. The tenter's business is to see
that none of the threads of the "warp" (the
threads running the length of the cloth) break.
The "knotters" at the knotting-benches tie

[1] Somewhere about 100° F.

knots in the fringes of towels, tablecloths, and quilts.' [1]

Beginners' wages range from 2s. a week in the spinning-room and 4s. 6d. a week in the weaving-shed.

Such a system is a palpable abomination. It is needless to enlarge upon its fatal effects, whether we regard the health and bodily development, or the intellectual attainments of the victims,[2] and whether we regard their present or their future. ' Whilst children are being taken in the factories, middle-aged workers are being driven out through an early collapse of the physical powers.' [3] An Inter-Departmental Committee reported on half-time in 1909, and strongly recommended its abolition, and this would have been accomplished long ere this but for the strong opposition in the districts concerned, which is responsible also for the fact that no progress has been made with a Bill introduced early in 1913 to put an end to all factory labour under the age of fourteen. Just as with the work of married women, half-time labour is *not* in the main resorted to on account of poverty. On the contrary many Lancashire weaving families have an income of from £200 to £300. But parents have themselves worked in the mills at a still earlier age, and cannot see that any evil results accrued to them. They have little faith in the practical value of school education, and think the youngsters might as well begin to pay their share towards the upkeep

[1] *The Social Workers' Guide* (Pitman).
[2] A Lancashire schoolmaster reported : ' A rapid and distinct deterioration is apparent in factory half-timers after a period of three months' servitude.'
[3] *The Millgate Monthly*, April 1913, ' Cotton Factory Children,' by James Haslam.

of the home. In case after case, when challenged, they point to some of the leading manufacturers of their own town, and say, ' You see it did him no harm, and what was good enough for him is good enough for our children.' When a ballot of adults in textile mills was held in December 1911 many did not vote, and 116,573 were against interference with the present system, while only 29,933 voted for raising the age to thirteen. At Burnley in 1909 the workers were seven to one against a change. All that is wanted to put an end to so barbarous a system as half-time is a more enlightened public opinion among these people, and any who will fearlessly go amongst them preaching the gospel of freedom for the children will render a service to the State. In Germany the lowest age for factory work is thirteen, in Switzerland fourteen. It is to our shame we tarry.

I have referred to the evil effects of half-time on physique, but would I could say that our educational house is itself in order in that respect. On this point there have been many searchings of heart among our educational experts during the last few years, and for my own part I may say I am convinced that education which gives little attention to physical training is to blame for much of the flabbiness of modern industrial life. It may be feared that school life, far from promoting physical development, is lived largely at its expense, yet it in nowise imparts qualities which will compensate for impaired physique when employment is sought. In fact the educational system of the day does not even seem to make for strong character, but rather the reverse, since manifestly a large proportion of boys and girls fail to learn ' to wish to live rightly,'

' and to acquire any love of wholesome kinds of physical and mental recreation.'

It is idle to assert that poverty alone is the main cause of impaired physique. Large numbers of extremely poor boys, for instance, from the west of Ireland are physically fit to join the Navy, though they have been accustomed to so poor a diet that for some time after they have entered the service it is said that many of them will even throw away some of the animal food with which they are provided. It is education that, when tried in the balance, is found wanting in so far as the development of physical efficiency is concerned; and the indictment surely becomes a terrible one when proof is adduced of the fact, which has been suspected by many, that the retardation of natural physical growth, which of course involves mental growth, has only too frequently been the effect of day-school life. Little children ought to be continually changing their positions and giving free exercise to all their senses, yet on attaining the age of five they are compelled by our law to sit still, frequently in crowded and ill-ventilated rooms, for considerable periods of time, and to remain silent except when answering questions. Professor Findlay of Manchester has found as the result of systematic weighing that it is chiefly during the holidays that growth takes place in the children he has examined, and various other tests go to show that the neglect of the physical welfare of scholars in the years when rapid growth is most natural is responsible for a great deal of physical trouble in later life. It is a hideous thought that any, let alone many, of the latest generation are by compulsion growing up delicate, stunted, crookedspined, weak-lunged, pigeon-chested, short-sighted —a hideous thought that after all our little ones might be better left undisturbed to play in the filthy gutters of the back streets. But, hideous as it is, it must be faced. Investigations by Russian, American, and German scientists show quite clearly that vigour of mind is in proportion to vigour of body; and in a little book I would recommend to all, and to which I am largely indebted for my information on this subject,[1] Mr. T. C. Horsfall, the well-known educationist and social reformer, contends that good physical training is a necessary part of really successful training for life. He argues from singularly convincing details that with the adoption of self-expression methods, and the giving of much more physical training, school life could be prevented from interfering with health and vigorous physical growth, while at the same time giving excellent mental and moral training, a large amount of useful knowledge, and a keen desire for a continuance of education. And he pleads for far more character-training than is to be found in the average school at present, this in its turn needing the highest character in those who act as teachers. ' Only if education succeeds in training to good character will its other results in scholars be worth their cost to the community.' Children must be taught— what, alas, many cannot learn at home!—to love, to respect, and to be happy.

The general feeling of apprehension regarding the physical condition of our population led to provision being made (1908) for the medical inspection of school children. The resulting investigations

[1] *Reforms Needed in our Educational System,* 1913, Barber, Manchester.

have amply justified the prevailing dissatisfaction, for a deplorably large proportion of children are found to be suffering from serious diseases or from ailments of the throat, eyes, ears, teeth, or skin. The natural corollary of inspection would seem to be the establishment of school clinics for treatment, but there is much divergence of opinion on this matter, and not many local authorities have yet got further than discussing it.   Up to July 1912 only eighteen northern local authorities had received the Board of Education's sanction for the establishment of treatment clinics, amongst these being Bradford, Grimsby, Halifax, Sheffield, and York, but not Leeds, Liverpool, Manchester, or Salford.

The importance of cleanliness in relation to health has been practically recognised in several districts by the installation of shower-baths in some of the schools.   These may be seen in Bradford, Darlington, Liverpool, Oldham, St. Helen's, Walsall, Warrington, York, and at the Manchester Country School for Town Children.

Another much contested point is that of the desirability of feeding poor children.   Whatever may be the evils of the system they cannot be so great as that of attempting to force nutriment into children's minds while their bodies are underfed. The co-operation of the School Medical Officers should always be enlisted (as is the case, e.g., at Newcastle-on-Tyne and Bradford), and the method of serving the meals should be educational.

An increased interest on the part of educational authorities in swimming is all to the good.   Many northern corporations grant facilities for school-children, and specially encourage them to qualify in ' life-saving.'   But until every child medically fit is taught this most healthy of exercises we should not rest satisfied.

The opening of certain city school playgrounds outside school hours is an innovation which has proved a boon to the children in crowded areas, and could with advantage be largely extended. Still more worth imitating is the example of the Manchester Education Committee, which last year made arrangements for the children of forty-five schools to visit parks and playing-fields with their teachers in school hours for the purpose of playing organised games.[1] Where the distances are too great for the children to walk, the Tramways Committee place trams at the disposal of the schools. The number of individual visits last summer was 97,000. If Ruskin made no mistake when he wrote, ' The entire object of true education is to make people not merely do the right things, but enjoy the right things,' the hours thus spent must be amongst the most valuable of the curriculum.

Playground classes, not uncommon now in country districts, are hard to arrange in cities, but where possible are a useful step in the direction of the universal open-air schools which are the ideal of the future. Schools in Blackburn, Halifax, and Sheffield have managed to overcome the difficulties and provide such classes. Bradford, Darlington, Halifax, Sheffield, and York maintain day open-air schools. The children in attendance show marked improvement in health. In 1911 the Halifax Education Committee opened in connection with

[1] In addition, the Manchester and Salford Playing-Fields Society, to whose initiative these arrangements are primarily due, provides instruction in organised games by lady ' games leaders ' in eleven recreation grounds in the poorest districts of the city.

its open-air day-school a residential open-air school of recovery, the first of its kind in the country. It provides for twelve boys and eighteen girls, and is very completely equipped. It stands five hundred feet above sea-level. ' The Halifax scheme as it now stands is wide and comprehensive, and can be made to embrace every class of weakly, delicate, or convalescent child of school age.' [1]

Whilst referring to Halifax I may mention parenthetically that it has for some years had a school newspaper called *The Satchel*. It is issued fortnightly and given to all scholars in the higher standards, who use it for their reading lessons and then take it home. The contents comprise athletic news, chronicle of events, gardening and natural history notes, extracts from English literature, calendar of famous events, short story, serial story dealing with local history, jokes, conundrums, etc.

Barnsley and Keighley have organised holiday schools or camps. Liverpool has a country school for physically defective children, which in summer is visited by selected small parties of children for a stay of three weeks. Far larger is the Manchester Country School which has been in existence about ten years, and now possesses eighteen acres of freehold land. It was provided by voluntary effort, but is under the control of the City Education Authority; three hundred and eighty children can be accommodated at a time, and some three thousand with their teachers are in residence each session. Forty children and a teacher is the usual party from one school. A child pays seven shillings

---

[1] *Annual Report for* 1911 *of the Chief Medical Officer of the Board of Education.*

for a fortnight's stay, and this meets the whole cost of maintenance and railway fare.

The Manchester Education Committee has, I believe, been the first in the country to recognise a Cripples' Day School. The school was started in 1911 at the University Settlement in Ancoats, and was taken over by the municipal authority in June 1913. About fifty children are in attendance. They are conveyed to and from the school, and are provided with dinner at 1d. a head.

CHAPTER V

THE ADOLESCENT

BLIND-ALLEY EMPLOYMENT—CONTINUATION SCHOOLS—CLUBS

THE subject of adolescent employment is of such fundamental importance that it is impossible to omit it from our present survey, though I feel it is somewhat superfluous to write of it here in view of the able monograph on *The Boy and his Work* in this same series. I trust that the few pages I can devote to the matter will be regarded as merely introductory to the valuable work of Mr. Spencer Gibb, or to that of Mr. Reginald Bray entitled *Boy Labour and Apprenticeship*.[1]

I hardly need explain that by blind-alley employment is meant employment which while offering fair wages to youths of from fourteen to seventeen, eighteen, or nineteen years of age has nothing to offer in the way of well-paid permanent work in later life. Such employment is that of the errand-boy, the junior clerk, the cart-boy, the youth who watches or feeds the mechanical appliances in many workshops, nut-and-bolt works, some electrical machinery establishments, etc.

It requires no previous study to discover that the result of the employment of this type of labour is

[1] Constable, 1911.

in no small degree responsible for much of the *unemployable* as distinguished from the temporarily *unemployed* population. For such occupations as those indicated are entirely uneducative. The whole mind and character of the boys, at the very time when they are most plastic, are allowed to remain unmoulded, and the glimmer of knowledge, and any desire for it which the last year in particular of school life may have kindled, are extinguished in a torpor from which there is grave risk they will never again spring to life. Thus it is that an enormous amount of the thought, the time, the energy, and the money expended on elementary education is simply thrown on the scrap-heap as the children leave school.

To say lightly that things will be all right if every boy be taught a trade, or, again, that what is wanted is the revival of apprenticeship, is to speak without a real appreciation of the facts. The problem is not so easy as that. In fact it is urgently demanding the concentration of the best brains of the country upon it as one which must be solved if we are to maintain our position among the nations. Year by year it becomes more serious. The few forces that counteract the evil are feeble. Continually the employment offered to youths is becoming more monotonous, and it is disheartening to consider that while intelligence is being awakened more widely in our undoubtedly improving schools, less and less are the opportunities for its application in most of the fields of labour in which the boy may find himself engaged. There is still great want of method in the general industrial training of children, and this though it is patent that dull, monotonous, uneducative work, work which often involves undue physical strain, for the three or four years of life in which body and mind are most impressionable cannot but be fraught with disastrous consequences for the whole of a lad's future. Cheap as may be the productions of the great labour-saving appliances, they are dear indeed to the community if their cheapness is only secured by the deadening of the intelligence and the atrophy of many of the finer qualities of youth. By what stages have we arrived at so deplorable a state of affairs ?

It will hardly be necessary to remind readers of the system of apprenticeship in vogue in the Middle Ages and later, with its strict supervision by means of the Trade Guilds. Under it the master assumed very much the position of a parent, and the boy lived in his master's house, learning every department of the trade he was to follow in later life.

With the advent of the age of machinery in the nineteenth century, involving a rapid and disastrous substitution of mechanical power for muscle and brains, there began one of the most shameful periods in English industrial history, a period in which little children were cruelly over-worked, and in which all thought of the people of the future seemed to be lost in the contemplation of the gains of the moment. To-day the country would stand aghast at the type of labour on which profits were then in no small measure based. It was not until 1833 that any Act of universal application was passed for the limitation of children's hours of labour, these being restricted to eight per day for children under thirteen, and to twelve for those between thirteen and eighteen. Eight years later a commission of inquiry into the condition of mines reported that young children were still harnessed to heavy trucks underground. The Factories Act of 1844 reduced the working hours of children under thirteen to six and a half per day; but Lord Ashley's struggle to secure a ten hours' day for 'young persons,' though he was supported in it by the Tories, failed owing to Liberal opposition. (See Spencer Walpole's *History of England*.) 'Some of the public men afterwards most justly popular among the English artisan classes were opposed to the measure on the ground that it was a heedless attempt to interfere with fixed economic laws' (Justin M°Carthy, *A History of our own Times*, chap. xiii.).

Space does not permit of my tracing the history of the many Factory Acts, which now more or less effectively insure the immunity from unhealthy conditions, from risk of accident, and from over-time labour of young persons employed in various occupations. The fact that never in a single Act apparently has the future of youth been considered at all is not unworthy of notice, for it serves to show that preparation for adult life has somehow been beyond the range of the vision whether of legis-lators or of their advisers.

In recent years the ever-growing use of labour-saving appliances has led to a marked increase in the demands of employers for mere boys. They are not wanted as apprentices to a trade, but merely as sentinels or guards over automatic machines to see that they are working satisfactorily, and fre-quently to feed them with the metal or other material which a few motions of the machine are to turn out a finished article. The work that such boys per-form is in no sense skilled, is not hard, and only rarely demands expenditure of either brain or muscle; but as it usually lasts eight or ten hours a day it is exceedingly monotonous, and appears in many cases to deaden the higher faculties, while at the end of the day's work there is an inevitable reaction which demands some form of excitement as an antidote to the life within the works.

Further, in many establishments no attempt is made to instruct youths in the knowledge of more than one machine; and even where this is done a boy who, for instance, has spent six years in some mechanical works may discover that some entirely new invention renders obsolete all that he knows.

Very frequently when a youth reaches eighteen years of age and asks for more wages, he is told that he cannot be advanced further, but if he likes to stay on at his present wages, well and good. He generally does not like, and leaves with the notion that he can quickly get another job, for he is totally unconscious of the harm which his mental powers have suffered during the previous two or three years. He finds in time that he knows practically nothing, that he has lost, indeed, what little knowledge he had, and that no one seems to want the *unskilled* labourer of his age, although constantly he may see advertisements appealing for young *skilled* workmen.

It is commonly supposed that youths who enter the textile trade are assured of employment in it for life. But the investigations of Mr. James Bell, the Supervisor of the Stockport Juvenile Employment Bureau, show that at any rate in the Stockport district early employment in the mill is often only of a blind-alley character. In the first annual report of the Bureau Mr. Bell states that ' a high rate of pay is given during the years of adolescence, and it is no uncommon thing to find boys of fourteen to fifteen years of age earning 10s. to 15s. a week. But while this high rate of wages prevails, and is thus effective in attracting boys into the mills, it is found that when the age of sixteen or seventeen is reached large numbers find themselves out of work. Of the 545 boys registered in the Bureau in twelve months, 132 were boys of sixteen and seventeen. The difficulty of dealing with these is due to the fact that (1) having been accustomed to a high rate of pay, neither they nor their parents are willing to accept less, even in a skilled trade ; (2) in most of the skilled trades apprenticeship must begin before the fifteenth birthday, unless the boy has had a secondary school education ; (3) the three or four years spent in the mill to a considerable extent unfit a boy for taking up work in the building trade, in iron and steel works, and in collieries, where boys of sixteen can be received.' [1]

Even worse in some respects is the lot of the huge number of boys who, fresh from school, become errand-boys, messengers, cart-boys, etc. Rarely can the errand-boy for the small employer hope to be retained as the years slip by, and although with the railway companies the case is different, the large army of cart and van-boys throughout the country have little prospect of adult employment. On the other hand these boys are not in so great danger of losing their vitality, individuality, and general intelligence, and if they will but change their occupation in time they are often little the worse for a year or two of a life which has at least the advantage of keeping them in the open air.

[1] *The Manchester Guardian*, January 9, 1914.

But sight must not be lost of the fact that as their callings do not come within the scope of the Factory Acts there is practically no limit to their hours of work, with the result that cart-boys in particular are often worked cruelly long hours—80 and 90 per week—and are denied any chance of improving their education even if they were to wish to do so. The recommendations of the recent Departmental Committee on the Hours and Conditions of Employment of Van Boys and Warehouse Boys should, however, if carried out, materially improve their lot.

In all the blind-alley callings little or no attention is paid to physique, and this, combined with the unhealthy conditions under which so many lads live, accounts for the illuminating fact that when they arrive at the age when they are out of work and are driven as a last resort, as thousands are, to try to enlist, a large proportion of them are rejected by the recruiting authorities on physical grounds alone. Sir Ian Hamilton has told us [1] that every year some 48,000 ' eighteen-to-nineteen-year-old recruits enlist because they have just ceased to be boys, and are unable to find regular employment. They come to us,' he says, ' because they cannot get a job at 15s. a week.' But well known as is this statement as a comment on our ' voluntary ' army system, what it really means is realised, it is to be feared, by but few. If 48,000 youths of the age named are accepted, all who have any knowledge of the matter will be aware that at least three or four times that number have applied and been rejected. To quote only one instance. In Manchester in 1899 of 11,000 young men who offered to enlist 8000 had

[1] *Compulsory Service,* 1910.

to be rejected, and of the 3000 left only about 1000 were fit for the Line. If at the present time army recruiting is still in anything like the same condition, it is evident that a very host of young men are year by year becoming unemployable because they cannot obtain work at a rate of wages that will keep them, and are physically unfit in the alternative to join either branch of the Service. For if we turn to the Navy, the symptoms are no less grave. It is stated that in order to obtain the number of about 5000 lads per year usually required by the naval authorities, 30,000 are rejected.

The immediate question therefore that faces the student is twofold : firstly, how to check the rush to blind-alley employment, and, secondly, how to improve the physique.

As regards physique, if any improvement is to take place beyond that which may be expected from improved housing and the diffusion of hygienic lore, it seems only possible by some method of physical training not only in the elementary schools, but after fourteen years of age. Provision for this might be made under a system of Day Continuation Schools with a curriculum including physical training, which a boy should attend for so many hours a week during the working day, the employer being compelled to release him for the purpose.

The answer to the first question is still less easy to find, though it may well be that the Juvenile Labour Exchanges, Juvenile Advisory Committees, and After-care Committees may do very much to insure that boys are placed in suitable employments when they leave school—' suitable ' meaning employments which shall so far as possible offer some prospect of an adult career.

It would appear that London, where the evil of blind-alley employment is most pressing, and Birmingham are more advanced in the organisation of such Committees than are the northern cities. In many, however, the matter is under discussion, and in some a beginning has been made. In Hull, for example, such a scheme was inaugurated in the spring of 1913 by the establishment of an Advisory Committee in connection with the Labour Exchange. The aim set before the Committee is to find for the children (about five thousand *per annum* in number) occupations suited to their abilities, and with good prospects, as they leave school; to try to induce them to enter Continuation Schools; to point out to employers the commercial advantages of having well-trained employees, and induce them to care for their well-being and health; and to advise parents as to the best arrangements for their children's future. It was determined to form a Registration Sub-Committee in order, with the help of the teachers, to interview the parents and collect information about the children before they leave school; an Employment Sub-Committee to inquire into trades and industries, and influence employers; and After-care Committees in connection with the schools to supervise and advise the former scholars.

In Bolton about the same time a conference was held with a view to arranging for an Advisory Committee consisting of representatives from the Education Committee, Trade Unions, employers, and others to relieve the situation pending the establishment by the Board of Trade of a Juvenile Labour Bureau, and later to co-operate with the Bureau. It was mentioned that the local Labour Exchange was haunted by youths of seventeen or eighteen, who, having started work with from 10s. to 15s. a week, were now only receiving 18s.

In Liverpool a revised scheme for carrying into effect the provisions of the Choice of Employment Act of 1910 by co-operation between the local Education Authority and the Labour Exchange was approved by the Education Committee in 1911, but in the event want of harmony between the Board of Trade and the Education Authorities has led to the setting up of two distinct Juvenile Employment Committees. Both appear to be doing useful work. That connected with the Education Committee is assisted by a strong Advisory Committee of employers representative of over thirty trades or associations. The provision of evening classes for nautical training to prepare boys engaged in blind-alley occupations for the Mercantile Marine is a departure worthy of special notice ; it is in effect the carrying out by a municipality of the idea originated by the late Marquis of Northampton for the placing in the Thames of a training-ship in which nautical education might be given to London boys engaged in some of the worst forms of blind-alley occupation, such as newsvending.

In Manchester some eight or nine years ago a Labour Bureau was founded in connection with thirteen Lads' Clubs, it having been found that where there were bureaux each in connection with a single club it was not possible to have enough boys available to make it worth while for an employer to apply. The experiment was not a success, and the club officials have found it best to do what they can to guide their boys to suitable occupation in an informal way. The city has only recently adopted the Choice of Employment Act, and has just formed a Juvenile Advisory Committee on lines somewhat similar to those of Birmingham. Salford had moved earlier than Manchester, and its Juvenile Advisory Committee is already responding to a long-felt want. Of course Manchester has long had a Juvenile Branch of the local Labour Exchange, but its work has not been very extensive, nor has it enjoyed the general support of the citizens. It must not be forgotten, however, that for many years past much has been done here as elsewhere by many of the headmasters and principal teachers to find suitable employment for their pupils when the time has come for them to leave school ; whilst the very considerable and entirely exceptional nature of the work of the various Lads' Clubs in this connection has done much to obscure the recognition of the real need for the setting up of an active and efficient Advisory Committee.

The greatest menace to the success of any Juvenile Advisory Committee at present is the extraordinary demand for boy-labour, which in our northern cities is in excess of the supply. This is leading parents to feel that they need not trouble about work for their boys, and is leading the boys themselves to discover the widespread desire for their services. Consequently neither parents, employers, nor boys care to trouble themselves about the Committees, and the familiar notice in the window or on the door of office or warehouse, ' Boy wanted,' is still the accepted method by which youths find employment and employers make known their needs.

With a view to preventing errand-boys and others who have taken unsatisfactory first employment from passing on as they grow older to further blind-alley occupations, the York Education Committee has recently (November 1913) approved a scheme ' for the establishment of day classes where English, arithmetic, woodwork, practical drawing, and mathematics will be taught. The scheme has been arranged in co-operation with a number of employers, who have agreed to allow their boys to attend classes four hours per week during working hours. No fees are to be charged. About a hundred boys will be in attendance.'

This is a move in the right direction. In Munich, where there are over fifty specialised Continuation Schools, there are also twelve district schools for young people not connected with skilled trades. Every boy is compelled to learn either woodwork or metal-work, and it is found that the training in these schools, and the acquisition of manual skill which it comprises, enables and induces many a youth to change from blind-alley to skilled employment. In 1909, for example, one of the general district Continuation Schools sent forty-one of its scholars into skilled trades.[1] It may be hoped that the York scheme will succeed in demonstrating how valuable the imitation of Munich methods might prove in this country.

Ultimately indeed the solution of the problem must largely lie in the revision of the national system of education. The best remedy, so far as can be seen at present, would be the raising of the elementary school age, combined with compulsory attendance at Continuation Schools. If boys did not leave school until fifteen, and then until the

[1] *The Continuation Schools in Munich*, by T. C. Horsfall, 1911 (Barber, Manchester, 6d.).

E

completion of their seventeenth year were required to attend day Continuation Schools, the curriculum of which included physical training for six or eight hours a week, the result would be to reduce the demand for juvenile labour, and at the same time to send up the wages of the adult worker.

At present I trust we may regard Continuation School education as only in its infancy, even in those cities which pride themselves, as does Manchester, on being the most advanced in the movement. If we consider very briefly what that city, as representative of the North, actually is doing, we find that out of a population between the ages of fourteen and seventeen estimated at about 40,000, only about 15,000 are continuing their education, the total number of evening students enrolled in the session 1911-12 being 24,563. This gives a percentage of only 3.44 of the population as against 2.08 for the whole country, though Manchester may congratulate itself in particular on the possession of its Municipal Evening School of Commerce, its Central Evening School of Domestic Economy, and above all its splendid Municipal School of Technology, which in staff and equipment is surpassed by none in the country. It was attended in 1911-12 by 5094 individual students, of whom 808 were enrolled in the day departments, while in addition 666 students attended summer courses. Government grants amounting to £13,000 were earned. Evening students attend three evenings a week, and the ' group ' courses of instruction are arranged to cover five consecutive winter sessions. A close connection with the Victoria University is maintained, and a large number of the students qualify for its degrees in the Faculty of Technology. The

Annual Report of the Education Committee contains the following suggestive paragraph :

> ' In the Session 1911-12 monthly reports were supplied to seventy-five firms dealing with 284 students attending evening classes or the day Apprentice Courses. The example of one large Company, whose head office is in the City, and which has established an " Education of Employees " Department, might well be commended. An official is appointed to take charge of the work, and promotion in the service of the firm depends in part upon satisfactory reports of the students' work in the School being received. In this way the closest co-operation exists between the School and the Company to their mutual advantage. Sixty employees, whose fees were paid by the firm, were in attendance during the session. Experience shows that fruitful results accrue where employers are willing thus to co-operate with the School ; and whilst the fact that contact is maintained with so many firms is encouraging, yet having regard to the extent of the industrial activities of the City and the surrounding district, and the large population employed, the proportion is really very small.'

Such records of magnificent uphill work as that from which I quote the above should go far to convince their readers of the impotence of even the most enlightened and energetic authorities to secure adequate continued education without the introduction by the State of the principle of compulsion, especially when we consider further the fact that for all Manchester Continuation School pupils the

hours of instruction work out at only 63 per year—
a lamentable figure when compared with the 330
hours of Munich pupils, though no worse than those
of other English cities.   What fine results might be
achieved with the same amount of thought and
activity on the part of the education authorities
plus a supply of students !

But whilst I am a strong advocate of compulsory
attendance at Continuation Schools, it is, I think,
essential that such attendance should be by day.
The best work cannot be done by boys and girls
jaded with the day's toil and unwilling to give up
any of their little leisure ; and it is right that
employers, who will derive benefit from the better
education of their employees, should be obliged to
arrange to spare them during working hours.   The
results of researches by Mr. W. H. Winch, External
Member of the Board of Psychological Studies of
the University of London and District Inspector
for the London County Council, into mental fatigue
among adolescent evening school pupils give
scientific support to my argument.   His tests
served to prove that evening work is comparatively
unprofitable, a short time in school in the evening
following on the labours of the day producing a very
low condition of mental energy.   The experiences
of the United States are instructive.   By a law
passed in the State of New York in 1910 boys
between fourteen and sixteen, unless they have
graduated in a certain course of study, are compelled
to attend school for not less than six hours per week,
or a trades-school for eight hours a week, for sixteen weeks each year.   The hours are from 8 to
10 P.M. on Monday, Tuesday, Wednesday, and
Thursday.   In the year 1911-12 of 21,000 boys who

should have been attending only about 7000 turned up, and the Superintendent of Schools himself admitted that he had not the heart to compel boys to spend their evenings in school after the day's work. In the Annual Report of the Inspector of Evening Schools the law is referred to as one ' approved neither by popular sentiment nor by the wisest educational considerations.' In Wisconsin, on the other hand, where since 1911 attendance for not less than five hours a week in the employer's time (day time) is compulsory for six months a year for all boys and girls from fourteen to sixteen, except for those engaged in agriculture, great satisfaction is expressed with the new law. It is the more notable seeing that in this State children under sixteen are only allowed to work forty-eight hours per week, yet the school hours must be taken from this time. Ohio also has compulsory day continuation classes, and others of the United States are discussing the question.[1] For the best examples of compulsory Continuation Schools we have to look to Germany, where as a rule they close by 7 P.M., and in particular to Munich, where under Dr. Kerschensteiner, Director of Education, who remodelled the schools in 1900, a wonderfully successful system has been evolved. The trades-schools, of which already in 1906 there were forty-seven, are highly specialised, and employers are very appreciative of the results of their work. Attendance for nine hours a week is compulsory up to the age of eighteen, by which time a large proportion of the students so well understand the value of education that they join the advanced schools for masters and journeymen.[2]

[1] *The Morning Post*, July 7, 1913.
[2] For further information on the German schools I would

Could an equally wise system of continued education, adapted to English needs, be devised for our own country there is no question but that we should hear much less of the evils of blind-alley employment, and that far fewer unemployables would be seen in our streets, prisons, and workhouses. It must not be expected, however, that we shall find in more education the complete and only solution of the difficulty. Education must be largely wasted unless the educated mind has opportunity for exercise; and the man, for example, who is condemned to make the same small portion of a machine, or a boot, or a window-frame day after day for life might conceivably not be much the better off at thirty, if he had attended classes to the age of eighteen or sixteen, than he is at present after leaving school at thirteen. If however he has been so well trained technically in his youth as to know the relation of his own small part of the work of a workshop to all the rest, and if in his leisure time he keeps his body vigorous and his mind well employed, the chances are that he will successfully resist the deadening tendency of monotonous toil. ' No doubt the present situation is due to the fact that we have not yet succeeded in adjusting ourselves to the vast change brought about by the introduction of machinery. How much adjustment will eventually be made it is difficult to predict, but it seems clear at any rate that so far the facts have not been sufficiently investigated.' [1]

strongly recommend my readers to consult the very valuable booklet by Mr. T. C. Horsfall referred to in the previous chapter —*Reforms needed in our Educational System.*

[1] Mr. E. A. H. Jay in *The Morning Post*, February 8, 1913.

With regard to girls it would be well for a beginning if it were made a condition of their being allowed to work in factories, that they should spend a certain number of hours every week in working time at continuation classes on housewifery, as must the employees of Messrs. Rowntree at York.

Pending drastic legislation for the prolongation of elementary school life and the establishment of Continuation Schools, probably the most useful agency devised for promoting the all-round welfare of the adolescent is the Boys' or Girls' Club. It is unnecessary here to refer to the various Boys' Brigades which along with Scouts flourish in the North no less than in the South; but the large Lads' Clubs of Lancashire are distinctive, and those of Manchester in particular are paralleled in no other part of the country. In Manchester and Salford over twelve thousand working-class boys are members of the chief clubs, about twenty-four of which form a Federation. Some clubs use premises specially built at a cost of £5000 or more, and several enrol over a thousand members *per annum*. The primary object of the club movement was the provision of places in which youths of the poorer classes, instead of loafing about the streets, might spend their evenings in congenial and innocent enjoyment, and be provided with opportunities for playing billiards, football, cricket, and other games. Success even exceeded expectation, and there can be no doubt that these institutions, along with the innumerable small church and chapel clubs, are to a large degree responsible for the disappearance from the streets of much of the hooliganism of twenty years ago. But it is now recognised, more generally, I believe, in the northern than in the London clubs, that they should aim higher, and that their activities should include the continued education of their members. Some of the largest and best evening schools in Manchester are those of certain of the Lads' Clubs, and Burnley Lads' Club school is also particularly excellent. Religious work on behalf of members unattached to any church or chapel is also undertaken by most of the clubs.

Such clubs afford a unique opportunity for young men willing to take up social work. The qualities most in demand are just those which are gained on the playing-fields of the great public schools, and the work itself is singularly encouraging and fruitful in results. The youth of the great towns are waiting for leadership and sympathy, and will respond to efforts to befriend them not only with personal loyalty, but often with wholly changed lives.

The similar work for girls is not on so highly organised and extensive a scale, but is altogether as desirable and as necessary, seeing that it is upon the mothers of the country that the future welfare of the nation depends. It is largely waste of work and energy to train the boys if the girls are left uncared for and untaught. Far more than is suspected are inefficient wives responsible for the misery of many back-street homes, and it is perhaps more than a coincidence that some of the Lancashire towns with the worst repute for their high rate of infant mortality have no girls' clubs within their areas.

I have already pointed to the useful work which may be done by clubs in guiding boys and girls to employments suited to their capacity and offer ing prospects for adults. To the man or woman thoroughly sympathetic and devoted to the interests of their boys and girls, there can be no more delightful experience than to place in good positions those whom they may see from year to year improving their prospects and profiting from the help which has been given them.[1]

I have said enough to show that the problem of the adolescent and his career is one which demands patient study, unwearying thought. But for a certain distance the right path is plain, and it is our reproach that public opinion has not yet forced our legislators to follow it. The terrible exploitation of the labour of little children in the earlier half of the nineteenth century is shameful to look back upon; but in those days the children had to work and use their wits, and many did become, strange to say, good strong men and women. The exploitation of juvenile labour to-day is taking another and a softer form, but I am not sure that the cruelty is not even greater; and that to kill the mental and physical activity of a boy just fresh from school, if not a worse, is a more insidious, form of cruelty than that of a period which every patriotic person now contemplates with horror.

[1] See my *Working Lads' Clubs* (Macmillan, 1908).

CHAPTER VI

OPEN SPACES AND PLAYING-FIELDS

In previous chapters I have sketched some of the problems that face those interested in the social welfare of the young of the northern cities. Now I must draw attention to still another problem which has only of late years begun to find recognition, and is only here and there confronted with some attempt at adequate solution.

Year by year as the great cities have grown up there has been added to their area street upon street of small tenement houses, north, south, east, and west, and these have been erected without any regard for the fact that plentiful air-space and opportunity for outdoor physical exercise are absolutely essential to the welfare of any community; and particularly for that of its boys and girls, who, unless they are able to take part in open-air games, must inevitably suffer in health and morals, and find an outlet in various unpleasant ways for the physical energy which is part of their nature. The greater the city and the more successful its merchants, the greater is the overcrowding in the centre, and the more obvious the want of thought for the health and happiness of those upon whose labour the very success of the place itself rests. The pitiful condition of what are known as the slum quarters of Liverpool, Manchester, or Newcastle, with their present horrors, would never have been reached had there been in the past any thought of an adequate town-planning scheme. I am convinced that much of the impaired physique of adolescents, which is so evident in any crowded area, is due to the want of fresh air and facilities for play ; and that the flabbiness and want of grit so often deplored are results of the failure to provide opportunities for acquiring the qualities of courage, good temper, and perseverance such as playing-fields offer.

How far indeed the lack of the provision of adequate open spaces and playing-grounds has a bearing upon youthful criminality, and therefore adult criminality—for it is the first offender who becomes the hardened criminal—it would be hard to say. It is significant that some years ago, when I was consulting Chief Constables all over the country with regard to the prevalence of juvenile criminality in their respective areas, one of them assured me that owing to the number of parks, recreation-grounds, and open moorlands available for outdoor exercise the youngsters in his district were giving the police very little trouble. And no less an authority than a former Lord Chief-Justice himself [1] has stated that ' Second to drink, and second only to drink, the real cause of crime is the difficulty of finding healthy recreation and innocent amusement for the young among the working classes.' It needs little imagination to realise that the want of open spaces and playing-fields lies at least at the back of much of what is generally understood by the term hooliganism, meaning the disorderly conduct of gangs of youths, who, having no facilities

[1] Lord Alverstone.

for play, make humble streets terrible for the
peaceable passer-by, and from acts of mere disorderly conduct may progress all too rapidly to
deeds of ruffianly violence.

Twenty-five years ago Manchester suffered much
from this kind of nuisance, known locally as ' scutt-
ling,' but there, as in Liverpool, the provision of
boys' clubs, with their encouragement of outdoor
sports and games, and the perception by many of
the leading citizens that it was absolutely necessary
to provide some means of recreation for the youth
of the city, has done much to reduce the evil.   In
recent years in fact the spread of enlightened views
among Manchester's municipal rulers has led to a
very large addition to the number of playing-fields
provided by the Corporation, while apart from
municipal action the Manchester and Salford Playing-Fields Society, founded in 1906, now controls
107 acres of land, providing accommodation for
about a hundred football and cricket pitches.   In
spite of this enterprise, however, there is not yet
anything like adequate provision of playing-fields,
and there remains the danger that even now vacant
land near the heart of the city may be snapped up
by the builder, and youths either be driven further
and further afield to obtain facilities for play, or be
deprived of all such opportunities.   Stockport has
recently imitated Manchester by forming a Playing-
Fields Society, which controls twenty-four acres,
and Bolton also has started a similar society, but
there is urgent need that the example should be
followed by other northern towns and cities ere it
is too late to secure land within easy reach of their
inhabitants at anything like a reasonable price.
For few places, unluckily, are so well off in pro-

portion to their population as is Newcastle with its 284 acres of parks and recreation-grounds, and in addition its ' Town Moor ' and adjoining grass-land amounting to a thousand acres.   It is no mere coincidence that the average daily population of Newcastle's gaol is less than one per thousand of the population of the city.[1]   It may be thought that I harp unduly on the connection between the want of playing-fields and crime, so I may explain that I take the statistics of crime as furnishing a pulse which we may feel to gauge the moral health of a community.   The same causes which produce criminals produce for every criminal hundreds of persons of impaired character, persons who are not such good citizens as they would have been but for these pre-judicial influences.   It follows that if the provision of facilities for play results in a diminution in the number of convictions, it results also in a raising of the general standard of character.

Naturally enough it is agreed that rough games such as football cannot be allowed in the public streets ; but it is a pitiful reflection on the social conditions tolerated in great cities that it is possible for boys of sixteen or seventeen, who may have been caught playing football in the streets, to be summoned before the magistrates and actually sent to prison for taking part in an absolutely innocent game, for the enjoyment of which there ought to be adequate opportunity.   The resort to extreme measures for the punishment of this offence against

Population, 1911		Average daily prison population, 1911
[1] Liverpool and Birkenhead,	878,891	1241
Manchester and Salford, .	947,804	1032
Leeds, ...	445,967	487
Newcastle, . . .	267,116	264

bye-laws is happily far rarer in the North than it appears to be in London, but that the law should be compelled to frown at all on a lad's instinctive pursuit of healthy development is lamentable.

The adoption of the Town Planning Act will no doubt prevent much evil in the future, but it cannot cure the condition of already crowded central areas. The only way in which this can be done at all is by the acquisition from time to time of old and uninhabited property, the demolition of it, and the conversion to the uses of a playground of the land so secured. An instance of this wise procedure has occurred at Manchester recently in the purchase from the War Office of the Hulme Barracks site of nearly eleven acres by the Corporation, with the intention of turning it into a playground for the most overcrowded district of the city. Such a policy may seem expensive to the shortsighted, but those with an eye for the future will realise its economy.

Men who are alive to the need for more football and cricket grounds sometimes damage their cause by failing to recognise the claims of little children and adults, who may find enjoyment and health on ground unsuitable for active games ; but it far more frequently happens that the value of playgrounds is overlooked in the struggle for more extensive parks, though the former are of at least as great importance as the latter. No better work can be undertaken by him who would endeavour to serve his fellows than to use whatever efforts he may be capable of to provide more breathing-spaces and playgrounds in the centre of great cities. Were their number multiplied it might be hoped among many other advantages that the needs of girls also would receive more recognition; and that the future mothers of the race, instead of gossiping on doorsteps, or wandering in twos and threes about the streets, would develop an interest in such appropriate games as basket-ball.

The gain to the health and general character of the young people of any city from a forward policy of this kind on the part of its municipality and social workers would be immeasurable. Not the least of the advantages obtained would be the check that such action would give to the spread of phthisis, for the germs of which overcrowding and darkness, the lack of fresh air and of lung-expanding exercise, form the most encouraging medium.

CHAPTER VII

HOUSING

DURING the last few years ' The Housing Problem ' has become a familiar expression, but no one who has failed to make some study or investigation of the subject realises its significance. Such an investigation should certainly be one of the very first matters to engage the attention of all would-be social reformers, for their efforts in every form of service among the very poor must remain largely fruitless so long as our industrial populations are compelled to live under unhealthy and degrading conditions. In fact, among all the many problems we are considering this is without doubt *the* problem. Its satisfactory solution would effect the reduction to a minimum of most of the others, for ultimately all our difficulties in crowded areas are concerned with health and character, and the influence of housing on these is supreme.

None will question this statement in respect of physical health; but if any be disposed to argue that people ought to rise above circumstances, and be clean, cheerful, industrious, and moral—as so many, wondrous to relate, are—regardless of material surroundings, I would ask him to exercise his imagination for a few moments. Let him imagine that he is condemned, not for a month, not for a year, but *for life* to live with his nearest and dearest in such a ' home ' as I am about to describe, and then let him dare to maintain that, whatever might befall his health, his character would not deteriorate.

No mere statement of the facts, however, even though it be read with the most imaginative sympathy, will ever carry conviction so far as will a personal visit to the mean streets of any city in this country, and the exploration of the interiors and back premises of the houses. The sights which may be seen on such a pilgrimage are absolutely appalling, and will leave the stranger wondering, not that there is so much evil, but that there is so little. For he will find in grimy, narrow streets and courts houses crowded together with practically no open air, through whose windows sunlight can never penetrate, with no yard-space at the rear where scullery and laundry-work may be carried on, and no possibility of through ventilation, with cellars used only as receptacles for filth, walls decayed and damp, covered in patches with several layers of dirty, peeling papers, falling ceilings that show mouldering rafters, roofs that allow the rain to drip on beds, broken staircases and crumbling floors, whilst a single water-tap out in the street may be shared by a dozen or more houses, and a single closet, in many cases not even a water-closet, situated very probably immediately beneath a bedroom, is all that is provided for the inhabitants of three or four, even of seven or eight, houses. To quote from the programme of the laying of the foundation-stone of some workmen's dwellings in 1910 :

' A typical Liverpool court (of which there were over three thousand prior to 1864) has been described as "a strip of land with a frontage of 30 feet to a narrow street by 60 feet in depth, abutting at the far end upon the high walls of warehouses or manufactories. Fronting and opening on to the street two three-story houses were built. Under the floor of one of the rooms of the front houses is a tunnel or passage 3 feet wide and 5 to 6 feet high to give access to the land in the rear. On this strip of back land, only 30 feet wide, are placed two rows of three-story houses facing each other with their backs against other houses, each with a frontage of 11 feet, and the same in depth including the walls; thus leaving barely 9 feet from window to window. Some sixty or seventy souls are crowded into this court having to depend for their breath of life upon this narrow well of stagnant air." In addition to this probably only two conveniences were provided, one placed at each end of the court, and in full view of all the residents of the court. A single stop-tap for water formed the only supply, and there was an absolute absence of air, and, of course, no yard-space whatever.'

Consider the following descriptions of homes in York :

‘ Courtyard. Entered by passage 4 feet, 9 inches wide. Yard partially cobbled. Six houses join at one tap and one water-closet. Five of these are back-to-back houses, and the sixth is built back-to-back with a slaughter-house. This slaughter-house (which has a stable connected with it) has a block of houses adjoining another of its sides, and the front of the building is separated from a row of houses by a street only 16 feet wide.'

' Courtyard. Houses all back-to-back. Yard cobbled and filthy. Ashpit overflowing. Water-supply for twelve houses from one tap placed in wall of privy.' [1]

Or these chosen at random from the reports of Manchester investigators :

' Two rooms. Rent 3s. 6d. Back-to-back house. Walls wet and structure in bad repair. Roof leaks. One tap in street apparently serves some fifty houses in this and next street. Six closets and one ash-place serve one side of street. Closets in filthy condition.'

' Two rooms. Rent 3s. 9d. House filthy. Tenant seems to be breeding rabbits in living-room ; nine or ten running at large on floor.'

' In one court there are three closets for eleven houses, but only one of the closets can be used, the others being entirely dilapidated.'

All this would be bad enough if, say, a four-roomed cottage were occupied only by one family, but not infrequently two or three families are the occupants. Again, take the following from the reports of the same investigators :

' No. 1 —— Street (typical of others in the street) is a five-roomed house occupied by four families (ten persons). Five houses share the closet used by the inmates of this house, and

[1] Seebohm Rowntree, *Poverty.*

twenty-two houses the water-tap, which is in the street. The house and tenants are very dirty.'

' No. 7 —— Street. House in very bad condition. Walls and ceilings damp and falling. This house has five rooms and is occupied by four families—fifteen individuals.'

' No. 20 —— Street. Two-roomed house. Invalid child in bed in bedroom, which is very damp. Water dripping from ceiling on to bed and floor. Wet patches in walls.'

Bedrooms in such houses very commonly contain but one bed, the linen upon which is not white but grey, the bedclothes in general often appearing to be a mere untidy heap of dirty rags. One does not care to imagine the scenes which must be presented at night when man and wife and possibly two or three children and a lodger are in occupation, nor the atmosphere which must be breathed, seeing that the window will be almost invariably kept shut to counteract the sensations of insufficient covering and damp. The cubic air-space will in instance after instance be found less than half that demanded by the Poor Law or by the bye-laws of the Local Government Board.[1] We find, for example, five sleepers in a bedroom of 990 cubic feet, six sleepers in a room of 865 cubic feet, and seven sleepers in a room of 1170 cubic feet.[2]

In Newcastle, a place whose death-rate compares

[1] Viz. 500 and 400 cubic feet respectively. I believe Professor Huxley said that in order to be supplied with respiratory air in a fair state of purity every man ought to have at least 800 cubic feet of space to himself.

[2] T. R. Marr, *Housing Conditions in Manchester and Salford*, pp. 63 and 69.

very favourably with that of other northern towns, over 10,000 persons occupy single rooms with an average of 4.2 persons per room, and over 81,000 occupy their dwellings at a rate exceeding two persons to a room.

Further, the cost of living in such places is by no means low. On the contrary, rents, considering the amount of accommodation provided, are positively extortionate.

It is unnecessary to point out that so long as dwellings of this horrifying type are allowed to exist, so long must drunkenness and vice play a prominent part in the life of crowded areas, so long must consumption claim thousands of unnecessary victims, so long must infants die like flies, so long must children suffer from all kinds of dirt-diseases, and grow into stunted, anæmic, hollow-eyed men and women.

It would be difficult to state in figures what is the direct cost to the community of the existence of slum-areas, but there can be no doubt that they are our most expensive national possession, and that to allow them to continue in existence is the falsest economy which any governing body can practise. It is chiefly the children from these districts who to the number of 18,000 fill our Industrial and Reformatory Schools, and to the number of over 200,000 are a charge upon the Guardians ; it is the adolescents and adults from the same quarters who make up by far the largest proportion of the inmates of our workhouses, hospitals, asylums, and institutions. From such areas the bulk of our prison population, amounting in 1911-12 to a daily average of 19,797, springs ; and it is in great measure because of such areas that we have to keep up our enormously expensive system of police, law-courts,

judges, magistrates, etc.   To all this add the huge
cost of charity—the remedial charity which provides asylums, ' homes,' institutions, schools, all
kinds of palliatives for the aged, the blind, the
crippled, the epileptic, the orphaned ; and the
preventive charity which strives to raise the lot
of the dwellers in these wretched habitations by
the provision of settlements, clubs, playing-fields,
lectures, classes, concerts, and the like.   And all
the time, whether we are paying taxes or subscrib-
ing to charities, we are but trying to fill a sieve with
water so long as the great Housing Problem is left
unsolved.   For better housing, and better housing
alone, is the *sine qua non* of any real social reform.

It is easy to decry the system which has allowed
slum-districts to grow up.   It is easy to rail at
those who profit by their existence ; who, however, in many cases are comparatively poor people
dependent on the rents they obtain.   But it is
extraordinarily difficult to find any rapid means of
effecting considerable improvement, though we
may at least hope that as progress is made with
town-planning the creation of such areas, which is
still going on, will become less and less common in
the years to come.   In our northern cities there is
at least considerable appreciation of the horrors
of the present state of affairs, and every patriotic
citizen, who will put the whole weight of his influence into the movement for reform, will help to
bring nearer a time when slum dwellings shall be
as obsolete as rushes on the floors of the well-to-do.

Liverpool awoke to the need of housing reform
in 1864, when its Sanitary Amendment Act was
passed, and the demolition of insanitary houses
has been going on since that date.   It was esti-

mated that their number was then 22,000, containing one-fifth of the population of the Borough. It
is claimed that no other town in the kingdom
possesses such extensive powers for dealing with
this kind of property as does Liverpool under the
Act of 1864. The city did not adopt the Housing
of the Working Classes Act till 1902. In 1896 the
Corporation decided that in future all Dwellings
erected by them should be reserved exclusively
for tenants who had been dispossessed, and it is
estimated now that eighty per cent. of the occupants
of the new Dwellings were formerly housed in the
demolished insanitary areas. In 1910 there were
under the Housing Committee's control some 2300
Dwellings, occupied by about 11,500 people. Some
description of one of the blocks of Dwellings, that
in Adlington Street, may be of interest :

They were opened in 1902-3, and comprise 48
tenements of one room, 70 of two rooms, 135 of
three rooms, and 18 of four rooms. The size of the
rooms varies from 14 ft. by 10 ft. 3 in. to 11 ft. by 9,
and their height is never less than 8 ft. Each tenement has a separate water-closet, and nearly all
have separate sculleries. Rates and taxes are paid
by the Corporation, and rents vary from 2s. 3d. per
week for one room to 6s. for the self-contained four-
roomed houses. A large enclosed playground is provided at the rear. The value of the land and cost
of buildings was £49,002, and the interest realised
through the rents is a little over three per cent.
The interest considered from another point of view
is much more remarkable. The death-rate in this
area, formerly notorious for outbreaks of cholera
and typhus, has dropped from an average of 50
per thousand to 27, whilst typhus has practically

disappeared, and tuberculosis, previously rampant, accounts only for 1.9 per thousand deaths. The birth-rate in the new dwellings is 51 per thousand.

Up to 1909 Liverpool had spent £980,739 on Demolition and Housing, and large schemes are still in progress to prove how well the importance of the matter has been grasped by the City Fathers. The most recently completed Dwellings are so built that should disease or vermin get in, a house can be ' stoved ' or washed down with a hose. Hot water is supplied to the inmates from a central station. The material used for three-story buildings erected at an estimated cost of about £100 per three-room tenement is concrete formed of crushed clinker from the refuse-destructors, with Portland cement. The sides, floors, and roof of each room are moulded in one piece, and only need putting in place on the sites of the buildings.

It was not till 1889 that the City Council of Manchester, as the result of reports from the Medical Officer of Health, decided to apply the provisions of the Artisans' and Labourers' Dwellings Improvement Acts (1875) to the worst areas of the city; but the work of re-housing in Manchester has been carried out mainly under a private Act of 1867, which, for example, provides that only twenty-eight days' notice of closing need be given to owners instead of six months under the Housing Act. Up to 1905 the improvement schemes cost the municipality £451,932 for the purchase of insanitary property, and the erection of Dwellings or conversion of the sites into open spaces. Included in this sum is £36,646 for an estate (Blackley) of 238 acres four miles from the centre of the city, purchased in 1899, of which 50 acres have been set apart for

allotments for the working-classes, and on which
150 six-roomed cottages have been built at a cost
of about £240 each. In addition, between 1885
and 1912 over 20,000 houses were ordered to be
closed under the Act of 1867, and of those actually
closed 12,954 were re-opened after a number had
been demolished to provide yard-space, and other
alterations had been effected. Owners were for
some years allowed a sum of £15 for each two-roomed
house demolished, yet the cost of administering
the Act up to 1905 only amounted to £35,500.
When houses are worth repairing and their owners
cannot meet the cost, the Sanitary Committee lend
them money for five or ten years at four per cent.,
the repairs being carried out by the Committee's
staff.

Other northern cities and towns are experiment-
ing with the housing problem on the same lines, but
even were the figures in every case available, it
would be to no purpose to go into particulars here.

In Leeds, where until quite recent times it has
been permissible to build the back-to-back houses
prohibited since 1844 in Manchester, a Limited
Liability Company, founded in 1876, has acquired
blocks of property in the more crowded parts of
the town, and, by judicious weeding of the worst
houses and careful management of the others, has
saved to the town as decent dwellings many houses
which otherwise would have been slum property.

This chapter would not be complete without some
reference to the undertakings of the owners of
certain large industries for the housing of their
employees in garden-cities on the lines originated
by Mr. Cadbury at Bournville. Port Sunlight, near
Liverpool, the property of Messrs. Lever Bros., and

Earswick, near York, founded by Mr. Rowntree, are the most notable examples in the North. Port Sunlight's houses and their surroundings, so far as these are dependent on man, are almost ideal, but ' the income from rents only covers the cost of maintenance and repairs, and does not yield any dividend on the capital invested. The head of the firm describes the scheme as " prosperity sharing "—the best means he can find of sharing profits with his work-people—and he has stated that the firm gets a return in the better health and consequent increased efficiency of the workers.' Earswick was built under rural bye-laws and laid out on economical lines, so that it has been possible to provide at a profit a cottage with a living-room 20 feet by 12 feet 6 inches, larder, scullery, three bedrooms, and a garden of at least 350 square yards, for 5s. per week. Hull, Manchester, Oldham, Sheffield, Warrington, all have ' garden suburbs,' but limited space forbids any attempt to describe these.

The foregoing sketch of what is being done in some cities of the North will have sufficed to show that broadly speaking there are three ways of dealing with insanitary areas and the housing problem, *i.e.* (1) the demolition of slum dwellings and erection of new houses on their sites at the cost of the ratepayers ; (2) the bringing of pressure to bear on owners to rebuild or improve their property ; and (3) the purchase by corporations or private individuals of land at a distance from the centre of a city for the housing of workers under semi-rural conditions. The reforms in Liverpool afford the greatest example of the first method, but when it is considered that the cost of rehousing has been £56 per head, whilst in Birmingham owners have been compelled to rebuild their houses in a satisfactory manner at a cost to the ratepayers of only 15s. for each person rehoused, the second method will be more likely to appeal to the impartial student. The third method is really in its infancy, but is likely to be far more resorted to in future, for as it is ' the poorest class of people are generally housed on the most expensive land. Cheap tram fares which would enable these people to live on cheap land would go far to solve one of the many problems of the housing question.' In this connection it may be noted that the Manchester Corporation paid £5, 6s. 9d. per square yard for the Oldham Road site in Ancoats acquired in 1889, whilst the land at Blackley cost about 7½d. per square yard ten years later.[1]

In considering the question of Housing, it is always necessary to bear in mind the possible effect of any large municipal scheme upon the wages of the workers for whom the accommodation is being provided, and also to guard against anything in the nature of undue monetary allowances to landlords or other property owners. There is a risk, and by no means a small risk, that if cheap housing accommodation were found for the people in the heart of great cities, the very fact of such accommodation being provided might cause the unorganised worker, so frequently to be met with in crowded areas, to be content, as one result of the over-supply of labour, to accept less for his labour than he had

---

[1] For the above particulars I am specially indebted to Mr. J. S. Nettlefold's *Practical Housing*, Councillor Marr's *Housing Conditions in Manchester and Salford*, and the Rev. H. Anson's pamphlet on *Housing Problems in Manchester*.

taken previously.   Any Housing scheme should be carefully watched in its application in order to see that what is given in one direction is not taken away in another.

The above is necessarily but a slight review of a very great subject, but will have made it clear that at any rate some municipal authorities are endeavouring — though they are endeavouring almost too late—to cope with the distressing evil of bad Housing.   But that they have grasped the principles of Town Planning in any comprehensive sense can hardly be said, for none of them as yet seems to look many years ahead.   An adequate scheme for the future of Liverpool, for example, would also provide for Birkenhead, Wallasey, Walton, Aintree, St. Helen's, Widnes, Garston, and other out-lying districts, whilst a proper scheme for Manchester should be formed in conjunction with the surrounding ring of towns—Wigan, Bolton, Bury, Oldham, Ashton, Hyde, Stockport, etc.   Much more might be done both for the immediate and the distant future were there only brought into the front rank of the attack upon existing conditions men of the type to whom I now appeal—men who have not always before them a narrow fear of increasing the rates, but whose imagination can vision for the future workhouses nearly empty, hospitals with numbers of vacant beds, prisons depleted of a great proportion of their population, industrial and reformatory schools evil dreams of the past.   Such an ideal is not beyond fulfilment. All that is wanted is that the labouring classes be provided with dwellings in which they can observe the sanctities of life, and which shall be homes in reality instead of the pestilential dens which so

often go by that name to-day.   Surely the people
who can sail among the clouds and navigate the
depths of the sea, who can penetrate to the Poles
and harness the hidden forces of Nature to their
tram-cars, are not to be baffled by mere darkness
and dirt !   The only real obstacle is that up to the
present darkness and dirt are not sufficiently hated,
and not hated by the nation at large.   Let but the
will to abolish them be there, and slums and slum-
dwellers will vanish like a nightmare at dawn.

CHAPTER VIII

AMUSEMENTS

THERE are few social workers nowadays who do not recognise the importance of recreation in the lives of humble folk. No longer is it common to hear music-halls, dancing-rooms, or boxing-saloons sweepingly condemned by people who have never been inside such places. No longer are ' penny readings ' or even ' lantern lectures ' offered as a substitute for ' wicked pleasures.' Yet it is hardly sufficiently realised how essential it is to have first-hand knowledge of popular amusements before making any attempt to influence or provide for the recreation of working people. Let me urge any practical reader to regard the remarks I am about to offer as merely an amateur's guide to the subject, and to make a study of it for himself.

It is to be feared that purely silly and sensational amusements are coming to play a much larger part in the general life of the community. Entertainments which require from the members of the audience some effort of mind in order that they may be fully appreciated are less and less in vogue. I may say at once, however, that in the North there is one very popular way of employing leisure time to which this criticism does not apply. Most of the northern communities are distinctly musical, and choral societies and instrumental bands flourish in a way which would arouse the surprise of many who are unaware of this characteristic. Take Manchester. Not only are Hallé's Orchestra and the Brodsky Quartette renowned throughout the country, but so in a less classical sphere is the Besses o' th' Barn Band, whilst a choir of mill-girls even goes on tour on the Continent. The great brass band contest at the Crystal Palace attracts yearly thousands of hardy excursionists from the North, who are content to spend nearly the whole of their day listening to the efforts of bands drawn in the main from Lancashire and Yorkshire, and many of whom are able to criticise the slightest mistake of any one of the instrumentalists.

So far as the musical instinct is concerned, there is little to cavil at, but it might often be supplied with better nourishment, and much more might be done in poor areas to bring something of the joy of music to the people's doors by means of what are known as ' court and alley concerts.' Such concerts have flourished in Liverpool and to a much less extent in Manchester, and have recently been promoted in Bolton by the local Playing-Fields Society. And rightly directed efforts to promote choral singing in even the poorest districts would meet, as has been proved, with a gratifying measure of success.

Against this entirely healthy interest in music there has to be set a keen delight in merely catchy tunes set to foolish and sometimes suggestive words, tunes which are devoid of all real harmony, but which linger for months, it may be for years, in the memory of those who hear them.

The music-hall indeed forms one of the most attractive of the amusements of the people. It may be said in its praise that to the development of the music-hall and the picture-theatre no little of the decrease in drunkenness is to be attributed, and that the performances, whatever they have been in the past, are to-day in the vast majority of cases innocuous. Sometimes they are spoiled by one or perhaps two ' turns,' as they are called, in which what is said or done is prurient. But it must be borne in mind that it is generally far better for a young man to visit a music-hall, and perhaps argue with his companion when he leaves as to how a particular acrobatic or conjuring feat is performed, than it would be for the same person to be standing loafing about some street corner, engaging in coarse conversation.

The music-hall has the advantage of being very cheap, and frequently whole families, father, mother, and children, may be seen seated there. But if it is not in itself the evil that it formerly was held to be, there is a danger, and by no means a small one, that it may become too engrossing a pleasure, and that for its sake money which is needed for home purposes may be wasted. There is another consideration. In some cases when parents frequently go to the music-hall alone, the young children are left at home uncared for, and lose much of that intimacy with the father which in most working-class families can only be obtained after the evening meal, and the absence of which is responsible for much of the ill discipline to be seen in towns and cities to-day.

Again, it must be remembered that the music-hall makes no demand upon any sustained thought. ' Turns ' follow each other with the utmost rapidity, serious succeeded by comic, and sentimental by tragic. The popularity of such a programme is only another sign of the restless spirit of the age, which for reading prefers ' tit-bits ' or any collection of snippets to the long-drawn-out tales of former days.

The same inability to concentrate attention is responsible for the fact that theatres in poor districts are not so numerous as they were a few years ago, nor do those that remain draw so well, however exciting the melodrama presented may be. This is probably due to the appearance upon the scene, as a third competitor, of the ' kinema ' or ' picture ' theatre. There can be no doubt of its potential value, and of the great educational use to which it may be put. But at present the character of the films shown requires very careful supervision. Everything depends upon them. Often they are excellent and instructive, but very frequently the plays shown upon the screen are merely the history of some burglary or other outrage against social order, exhibiting episodes of all kinds, and pandering to the taste for sensation which is so much in evidence on every side. This, of course, is the cheapest of all forms of entertainment, since for a penny or two a couple of hours' amusement may be enjoyed, as well as a rest in a comfortable chair, a consideration which considerably adds to the attraction of the theatre for adults, especially for women.

Both music-hall and picture-theatre usually arrange their entertainments so as to give two performances a night, from 7 to 9 and 9 to 11. In certain districts it is noticeable that to an extraordinary extent the entertainments are patronised by young people. So much so, indeed, that the efforts of educational authorities throughout the North are being more or less hindered by the attractions of such places, whilst physically the children are harmed by being deprived of a proper amount of sleep. Action has been taken recently to mitigate this evil, and in Manchester, Salford, Liverpool, and other towns young persons apparently under sixteen (in some cases fourteen) years of age are by bye-law prohibited from attending the later entertainments, except when accompanied by adults. It is likely that children suffer also from the stuffy atmosphere of the theatres, and from the strain upon their eyes. The fascination which the films possess for many older persons is harder to understand ; though when their children are old enough regularly to spend their evenings away from home, at clubs or classes or theatres, it is not surprising, or a matter for deprecation, if the parents, and more particularly the mothers engaged in home drudgery all day, seek a change of scene. I know a highly respectable widow, the mother of grown-up sons, who makes a regular practice of going to a picture-theatre, or sometimes a music-hall, five nights a week, and I understand there are many like her.

Among young people dancing is popular, but unfortunately it is a pleasure indulged in generally under exceedingly harmful conditions. There can be little doubt that to its dancing-rooms may be attributed much of the immorality of many a district. Here is an opening for the social reformer. Dancing is the expression of a primitive instinct, and to condemn it as so many do without reservation is both foolish and injudicious, since all who have any knowledge of the young know quite well that what is forbidden and condemned is sought after.

Dancing is certainly not necessarily immoral, and, if properly conducted, it confers much happiness and brightness in the poorest districts. Where the exercise is not frowned upon, and where young people are encouraged to meet and enjoy themselves in this way, the proceedings are usually absolutely unobjectionable; but where parents forbid the exercise as ' wrong,' and boys and girls surreptitiously frequent low dancing-saloons, the results are deplorable. The recent movement for the teaching of Morris dancing and of old English folk-dances, with their natural grace, is much appreciated and deserves encouragement.

Among more modern amusements whist-drives must not be forgotten. These are an excellent innovation in working-class districts, for they are not occasions for meetings of members of one sex only, but are almost invariably gatherings of both men and women, youths and girls, who, to the number often of two or three hundred, for a small charge play for certain prizes which usually take the form of some useful personal or household article. Nothing is more needed than for both sexes to meet in this way on common ground, and the success of the whist-drive should be an example for the organisation of other gatherings where the sexes might meet with similar gaiety and decorum.

As regards outdoor amusements I have already referred in Chapter VI. to the great need of additional playing-fields and open spaces, and it is not necessary to refer again to that aspect of the question.

So far as boys are concerned, there can be no doubt that in the north the game *par excellence* is football. From the days when they begin to go to school this is the one game which most absorbs their attention, and it continues its exclusive claim very often until they are well over twenty years of age.   In courts and alleys, on vacant plots of land, on brickfields, indeed where any open space at all may be found, attempts are made to play the game, even although the football be but a bundle of tightly rolled up, string-bound papers.   Small clubs spring up on all sides, financed in extraordinary ways, but in all cases deriving the bulk of their income from the actual payments of those who take part. Various leagues, as they are termed, are formed, and keen competitions for ' championships ' are engaged in throughout the season.   The casual observer might well think that here at all events in junior football is an activity to be unreservedly commended.   But, alas! the standard of honour among the players is frequently but a low one. Where leagues are formed for youths of a particular age it is a common practice for those of a higher age to lie and cheat in order to join, and so endeavour to make certain of winning whatever trophies may be offered.   The play itself is frequently unfair, and too often foul and violent tactics take the place of strenuous play.

Here is a splendid field for the young man fresh from public school or university.   Familiar with games himself, and imbued with a high standard of fair play, by organising a football team and taking a close interest in those who are its members, he may do much to raise the whole standard not only of play but of life.   For something more than sportsmanship is involved, and that is character. For many months of the year his weekly football match absorbs a very large proportion of many a boy's capacity for interest in life, and if the game which seems to him of such paramount importance is in any way associated in his mind with dishonesty and untruthfulness, it is almost inevitable that the taint will spread and affect his conduct, or at least his judgment, in other matters. Possibly the Football Association could do something to improve this state of affairs by endeavouring to supervise the formation of all leagues, and by making rules to provide as far as possible against cheating in the matter of age. But nothing the Association could do would be so effective as the influence of individuals in charge of institutions such as Sunday schools, who with eyes open to this evil might do much to check it by insisting that their lads should as a matter of course produce their birth-certificates, and by giving more personal consideration to the nature of the leagues they allow them to join. Still more desirable is it that they should use their influence to reduce the foolish medal-worship which is the curse of youthful athletics, and urge the members of their teams to care more for clean games and honourable victories than for paltry scraps of silver to hang on their watch-chains.

It is the correct thing nowadays to decry the practice of vast numbers of youths being spectators of football matches rather than players. Little do many of those who so loudly raise this plaint realise that most lads would far sooner be playing than watching. If circumstances over which they have no control render playing-fields inaccessible for them, it is on the whole far better that they should be watching a game which they understand rather than be roaming the streets idly, or (if they are over about twenty-one or twenty-two years of age) spending the Saturday afternoon in billiard-hall or public-house.

In summer cricket easily holds the first place, though it is by no means so popular a game as football. Here again much may be done by a man who has keen interest in the game. Just as in football unfair tactics are often adopted, these being particularly noticeable in wicket-keepers, who consider themselves, and are often considered to be exceptionally smart, if they can manage to break the wicket with their pads so as to cause the batsman to appear to have been bowled.

One great outdoor amusement of the people must not be omitted from this survey, and that is the cult of the Sunday evening parade or walk. In every city some few of the principal streets are marked out as the resort on that evening of the week of all who possess Sunday clothes. Footway and roadway are alike taken up, and crowds, on the whole merry, pass up and down for some two hours. Both sexes take part in this parade, usually in little knots of three or four or more boys or girls. Sometimes there is an element of roughness, sometimes there is a measure of disorder, sometimes a considerable degree of coarseness in the remarks which are passed. On the other hand there is much harmless enjoyment, and the parade provides the great opportunity for the making of new acquaintanceships, which often blossom into friendship, and not infrequently end in marriage. The opportunities for the sexes mingling together socially are so rare that no surprise need be felt at this apparent rebellion against the ordinary trammels of life. The problem is not so much to decrease for young people the opportunities of meeting, but so to raise the general tone and character of the people themselves that what is harmful should be eliminated, and the impression be gained that social fellowship may be enjoyed equally well apart from the crowded parade street with all its noise and distraction.

'Of other amusements there is no space here to take individual account, but photography, fishing, walking, bicycling, bowls, and various indoor games all have their devotees. Given a sympathetic lead in these directions not a little may be done to raise very materially the general level of recreation. Temperance billiard-halls abound in northern cities, and have done much to dissociate billiards from the public-house. With the same object of leading men and women to find their amusements apart from drinking, a variety of clubs and institutions have been founded with more or less success. I have already alluded to the Middlesbrough Winter Garden. The David Lewis Club in Liverpool, established in 1902, is the largest place of the kind. ' It has no religious basis, and the work falls naturally into two departments, educative and recreative. The latter side of the work predominates, and is conducted by means of dances, whist-drives, chess, draughts, billiards, football, swimming, and boxing, and on one occasion per week a theatrical performance is arranged.' [1] It is of interest to note that the works of Galsworthy and Shaw, Ibsen and Wilde, are appreciated by the dock-labourers. The management of the club is democratic, the House Committee consisting of twelve popularly elected members.

[1] *Palaces for the People. A suggestion for the Recreation of the Poorest People*, by F. J. Marquis, M.A., and S. G. T. Ogden (1912).

A meeting was held in Liverpool in February 1913 to discuss a scheme for establishing, if possible with the support of the civic authorities, ' palaces ' for the recreation of the poorest inhabitants. Some supporters of the movement are in favour—wisely, I think—of the experiment of allowing the sale of light alcoholic drinks with a view to attracting people of a lower caste than the frequenters of existing ' people's palaces.'

In this connection I cannot omit to refer to the Ancoats Recreation Committee in Manchester, which provides at a charge of 6d. or 1s. the finest classical concerts given in any working-class district in the country ; and at no charge at all Sunday and week-day lectures, often by eminent men, on every variety of subject, enlivening these occasions also with good music. The organisation of ' at-homes,' reading-parties, summer rambles, and even trips to the Continent, and the endeavour to promote the appreciation of beauty in all its forms, whether in Nature or Art, are characteristic of this unique and highly successful society. It was founded thirty-seven years ago by Mr. Charles Rowley, who is still the heart and soul of its activities. Born in Ancoats of lowly parentage, he is now one of the leading citizens of Manchester.

No account, however brief, of the amusements of the people of the North would be complete if it did not contain reference to the custom of an annual holiday, usually termed the ' Wakes ' or fair-week. The origin of the holiday and its name date back to very early times, when it was customary to celebrate the vigil or eve of the day sacred to the saint to whom the parish church was dedicated. This holiday period in the various manufacturing towns usually occurs between the end of June and the end of September, except in Manchester, where such general holiday as does exist is taken in Whitsun week, and in Liverpool, which has no such general holiday at all.

In the purely manufacturing districts the Wakes week, when all the mills stop, is the great event of the year. To furnish the means for its enjoyment it is the practice of many work-people to lay by money week by week, and entrust it to officials of many of the mills and foundries, who undertake to bank it for them until the eve of the holiday. Money is also saved by means of clubs run on very much the same lines as the ' slate clubs ' of London. The amount of savings withdrawn by inhabitants of the Lancashire towns in preparation for the Wakes of 1913 amounted, it is estimated, to over a million pounds.

The most pleasing characteristic of these holidays is that it is not only the men who take part, but as a rule whole families. From Burnley, Blackburn, Colne, Preston, Oldham, and indeed all the chief towns in Lancashire, a very large proportion of the total population once a year migrates to Blackpool, Douglas, Rhyl, Morecambe, and other seaside resorts, there to enjoy a week of unalloyed rest and pleasure. The amount sometimes spent by such families on their holidays is very large indeed, but the holiday is often made the occasion for the purchase of new clothes and other necessities for the year, and on the whole expenditure is on innocent enjoyment. There cannot be any doubt that very great benefit to the general health of the community results from this custom.

To those who do not leave their town when the

annual Wakes come round, there is open the enjoyment of the ' fair,' which is usually established on the market ground, and is composed of a collection of the booths of travelling showmen. Here, night after night, young people and their elders resort to delight in ' cokernut-shying,' the trial of various feats of strength, rides on ' scenic railways,' and indeed ' all the fun of the fair.'

Recently there has been a tendency in some of the towns whose Wakes are early to take in addition a long week-end holiday in September. Bolton, for example, thus secures a total of eleven days' special holiday in the year.

suffice to divert its adherents to other things. While this cannot be done, however, it is nevertheless possible—indeed it is an obligation—to protect people to some extent against themselves, and much may be accomplished by the social reformer in seeing that the enactments of the law are carried out, and in promoting such legislation as Lord Newton's Betting Bill.

It is hopeless, however, to look only to repressive legislation as a means for bringing about a diminution in the prevalence of excessive gambling. Like every other evil it is the effect of causes, and these it is the first necessity to discover and war against.

Betting upon the results of athletic contests and games of skill has always existed, and will always continue between persons interested in such competitions. The real interest in such bets is the game itself, the prowess of an individual or a team, the desire emphatically to express faith and loyalty. The sordid notion of mere money-making is rarely even a secondary thought. But to gamble at the risk of money which he who stakes cannot in any sense afford to lose, and which often he cannot even pay when he does lose, upon the results of competitions in which he has no interest of any kind except so far as his money is concerned—this is something entirely different.

While the gambling fever is undoubtedly in the poorer sections of the community a reflection of the general insensate greed for money, and for pleasures which can only be purchased by money, to any one familiar with life in great industrial centres and acquainted with the social habits of the people, it will be well known that the contented man does not gamble. In other words men who are paid

what they consider to be a fair return for their
labour, *i.e.* a sum which will enable them adequately
to maintain their homes and provide for their
children, do not as a rule recognise any appeal in
the most attractive tipster's circular. For adequately remunerated men, whether their work be
manual or clerical, gambling is an exceptional vice,
and generally is the effect of other causes than those
I have in mind, causes for example which have their
origin in domestic unhappiness of various kinds, and
in a complete failure of the so-called education of
early years to attract the mind to what is good and
noble in life.

Nothing is more unjust than to assert of working-
men as a body that the gambling habit is only one
form of expression of a generic viciousness. As a
matter of fact the underlying cause of the habit
is in case after case but an attempt to rebel against
economic conditions. Men and women innumerable have fallen into the morass of gambling from
a perfectly innocent wish to supply for themselves
and for their offspring the necessities of life which
the poor reward of their labour fails to provide.

The low-paid labourer with a sovereign or twenty-
two shillings in his pocket at the end of the week,
if he reads or thinks at all, and is the father of a
family, knows full well that his earnings do not and
cannot suffice to maintain his wife and children in
decent health, even without the smallest provision
for holidays or enjoyments of any kind, and—
which weighs in the mind of a working-man far
more than is generally supposed—without his being
able to provide for an encounter with the common
disasters of life, sickness and unemployment. To
some extent the Insurance Act now enables him to

cope with both these troubles, but not fully, and he sees before him a long vista of years of constant struggle, and at the end, if he predeceases his wife, no provision for her in the years that may yet remain.   He sees ever more clearly the widening gulf between himself and those who employ him, the growing display of luxury on the one hand contrasting with his own wretched condition on the other.   The feeling arises within him that in some way he must improve his material surroundings.   How he knows not.   Nowhere will his rough, unskilled labour be paid at a higher rate than he is receiving.   Yet he feels that the few pence an hour paid for strenuous toil, for straining muscles, for aching back, and perspiring limbs are not an adequate share of all that his efforts bring to his employers.   There comes before his eyes the bait of an alluring circular from the racing tipster, or the advertisement of some speciously easy newspaper competition promising to the winner every week for life probably considerably more than his present wages.   As he reads and gives rein to his imagination the printed words bring before him almost the certainty of obtaining that increase of material things which will make life easier for himself and his family, and make it possible for them to live it more as he knows it ought to be lived.   It needs but the expenditure of sixpence or a shilling, and a prognostication of the result of some race, or match, or competition, which in his complete ignorance of mathematics appears to him so simple to get right.   At the least the price of some much-needed additional food or clothing or some longed-for day's outing may be won.   The hope of obtaining money in this way is one but rarely gratified, but once a start has been made the gambler feels unable to call a halt. Indeed, among many who find in gambling their sole amusement, the attraction is not so much the possibility of winning money, much as it may be needed, as the actual excitement of the risk of sums which the gambler cannot afford to lose, an excitement indulgence in which affords an unhealthy expression for energies which have been kept absolutely damped and unexpressed while he has followed some monotonous employment during the busy day. The increasing use of mechanical labour-saving appliances is, I fear, making the monotony more marked ; while at the same time the worker is continually being ' speeded up,' or in other words required to see that the machine over which he stands sentinel turns out more and more per day of the articles which it has been planned to make.

Most deplorable of all is the spread of the gambling pestilence amongst women. The subject is one of the highest importance, for it may be that in the growth of this habit lies the cause of the increased drinking habits of many women. Indeed, I am inclined to think that if any additional force had been needed for the opening of a door to the acquisition of the drinking habit by women, it would have been supplied by the realisation by innumerable women that gambling is something which not only men, but they themselves may indulge in. Gambling among women has in it the elements of greater social danger than when indulged in by men, for women never bet on account of their interest in horse-race or football-match, but invariably for the sake of gambling—simply to get money.

No one familiar with life as it is lived in the dark places of the land can have failed to discover that it is not the men and youths only who are the customers of the back-street bookmaker, but that his *clientèle* is increasingly drawn from among the poor women of a district, who in their desperate efforts to win money do not hesitate to exchange with the pawnbroker for a few paltry coins the very necessaries of their homes. Frequently the craze which has seized upon his wife is unknown to the husband, and for a time, until the inevitable disclosure is made, a system of organised lying and hypocrisy, and sometimes of stealing, is resorted to, not perceived indeed by the trusting, unsuspecting man, but often enough seen and understood by children. Thus early in life they may become familiarised with much that all unconsciously to themselves becomes the polluted source of the adolescent want of candour and truthfulness which is so much deplored at the present time.

Mere statement of facts, for they are facts, such as these may reasonably enough carry no sense of conviction to the reader. Therefore, I make no apology for quoting the following from the *Annual Report of the Manchester City Mission*, one of the oldest and most influential missions in the country :

> ' Children's clothes are pawned for money to bet with. One woman, with seven children, begged for money for the children's dinner ; she got sixpence, and then " put it on a horse." In another case, while the missionary was praying in a house, the boy came to the door with the sporting paper ; the woman got up from her knees and bought the paper, though

she had just said that she had nothing to buy food for the children. Her excuse was that she wanted to win. Sometimes the women sublet a room to the bookies, who pay them one penny for every shilling made in bets. One bookie was prosecuted for this and fined £100, and he was glad to get off so well. A broken-hearted father came to the missionary about his boy, who had not come home all night. The boy had sold eight shillings' worth of papers, had gambled all of it, and at last came home without a penny. In a certain part of one district, every day between twelve and two o'clock the bookie may be seen, or sometimes two or three of them. The missionary, standing for fifteen minutes one day, counted forty-eight men and women who came to make bets with the bookies. On another day forty-three women were waiting in groups to know what they had won, and every one of them had lost.'

Mr. H. Beecher Cooke, the Organising Secretary of the Lancashire, Cheshire, and District Anti-Gambling League, in a recent interview stated that there could be no doubt of the very serious increase in gambling among women. In Blackburn, Burnley, and Rochdale, for example, nearly every mill, he said, is infected with the gambling evil, usually taking the form of sweepstakes on horse-racing and football. In a back street in Ardwick, a district of Manchester, twenty or thirty women, many of them mothers, were found waiting between ten and eleven o'clock in the morning for the ' tipping sheets.'

H

'The bookmakers themselves,' remarked Mr. Cooke, ' are not often seen. Usually a woman acts as the bookmaker's agent on commission ; sometimes for a man bookmaker, sometimes for a woman bookmaker.' Reverting to gambling in mills and workshops, he said that a lot of the bookmaker's work was done through foremen acting as agents. ' Frequently,' he observed, ' young people come to me and say, " It 's awful at our place. The foreman is a bookie." The result is that many young people are almost forced into gambling, for if they don't do what the foreman wants they get into his " bad books," and have an uncomfortable time.' As an example of how gambling amongst women causes domestic misery Mr. Cooke said, ' One day, while waiting for a car in Salford, I was reading a newspaper, when a little girl came to me and asked, " Please, sir, what 's won ? " On inquiring why she wanted to know, she replied, " It 's my mother." I then went with her to her home, if it can be called such. There was nothing in the house but a table and one or two broken chairs. The woman had six children, but I found that every article possible had been pawned by her in order to get money to put on horses.' He went on to say that he knew of many working-women who had bet anything from eight shillings in a single day. They got the money by pawning and borrowing.[1]

My own experience goes far to confirm what was stated by Mr. Beecher Cooke. There can be no doubt in the minds of those interested in the welfare of growing children that much of what is so constantly criticised in them—as decay of filial obedi-

[1] This information was given to a representative of *The Manchester City News.*

ence, dislike of restraint of any kind, unrestricted licence as to the manner in which leisure time is spent—is but the natural outcome of a diseased and unnatural taste for the excitement born of gambling usurping in their mothers' hearts the place of love of home and ever present regard and thought for the little ones within it.

How is it that the craze for gambling so rapidly gains a hold upon women ?

No one with any experience of mean back streets can fail to be impressed with the deadly monotony, the loneliness, drudgery, and want of beauty in the lives of the women during the long hours of the day, particularly of the morning and afternoon, when the children are at school and the breadwinner away at work. It is amazing in how few years the bright young wife may become the slatternly, unclean, nagging, shrill-voiced occupant of a back-street doorstep ; in some cases, owing to her unseemly attire, for years hardly moving outside the area of her own small street, unable to contemplate a holiday, unable to purchase new clothes, her life one continual round of endeavouring to make both ends meet and keep the home together. To such a one suddenly there comes the news that Mrs. Brown has won fifteen shillings on the ' Lincoln,' and has bought a new blouse, and some pictures and curtains for her parlour—' and all for a shilling !' Mrs. Brown had read in the paper that ' Red Fly ' was sure to win, and had put a shilling on just to try her luck.

Mrs. Jones, distracted with worry as to how she is to find a new Sunday suit for her eldest boy, sees here a way by which she too may profit. Eagerly questioning her neighbours as to the next

big race, she is told that the *Daily Sun* says that
' Blue Pilot ' cannot fail to win the great event
next Friday. ' But,' she says, ' I 've no money.'
' Well,' the tempter answers, ' why not pawn your
best boots ? ' Poor soul, her ' best boots ' are but
a caricature. Yet a shilling may be obtained upon
them, and without hesitation the plunge is made.
Alas ! ' Blue Pilot ' does not win, and when Sunday
comes and Mrs. Jones should go for a little stroll as
is her wont, she stays at home, telling her husband
that she does not feel so well. On Monday she seeks
counsel with her neighbours, saying that she must
get her boots by the week-end, or her man will find
out she has pawned them—and again she plunges.

No need to pursue the tragedy further. Either
more and more is pawned and lost, or success
attends a bet. If the latter, the good luck has to
be celebrated with the neighbours, and for the first
time in her life, perhaps, Mrs. Jones stands treat at
the corner public. A little time passes, and all is
discovered at home. But by then the mischief is
done. She has become a gambler, and her husband,
pleading or wrathful, can do nothing to check her.

It is unnecessary here to enlarge further upon
the gradual effect of excessive gambling in the home,
whether the practice of mother or father or both.
Every worker among the poor has observed the
pawning of household effects, the occasional placing
of a whole week's wages upon some fancied horse,
the beastly carousals that so often follow a winning
stake, the gradual decay of whatever ideals the
family may have had. None will need convincing
that this craze, this curse of gambling, is inflicting
upon the community an amount of wretchedness
which cannot adequately be expressed in words.

It will be well known to my readers that the
gambling mania has lately made extraordinary
advances, especially in Lancashire and Yorkshire,
by what is known as the coupon betting system in
connection with the national game of football.
Apart from mere medal-hunting, it is only in recent
years that thoughts of gain have become connected
with football. Of course as with all games there
have always been the odd sporting bets between
one keen partisan and another, but these have
never done much harm. Some years ago, however,
among junior teams in the North there sprang up
with great rapidity a system which was called
'making a book.' This really meant getting up
a sweepstake upon the result of an important local
match. A boy would head a page of a grimy little
book, say, 'Liverpool v. Sunderland,' with the date,
and below would be lines for entries providing for
wins for either side up to possibly six goals and a
draw. A penny a share was the usual charge, but
several shares might be taken by one boy. If
fifteen shares were issued, the winner would receive
a shilling, so that the promoter would gain threepence, or in the event of more than the six goals
being scored would pocket the whole one shilling
and threepence. This form of gambling spread
very quickly among boys, and soon more compli-
cated 'books' were devised and larger sums became
involved. In March 1905 we find *The Manchester
Evening News* condemning the 'new evil' of the
coupon system in the following words :

> 'Newspapers catering for football, and
> presenting coupons for prizes value anything
> up to £1000, have whetted the public appetite

for an easy way of gaining wealth, and the present evil, which has developed rapidly, is the natural outcome. Bookmakers, ever ready to pick the pockets of working-men, do not object to pick the brains of *confrères*; and a " system," founded, we believe, by a Liverpool bookmaker, has made its appearance in every large town in Lancashire. Liverpool, Wigan, Bolton, Manchester, Horwich, Blackburn, Accrington, each possess " bookies " willing to lay odds in accordance with this system. This new and dangerous form of betting is rapidly spreading, and threatens to become as big a source of income to the " bookies " as the " starting-price " betting on horses. Working-men are captivated with the idea, and the " bookies " are doing a roaring trade amongst the artisans of the great engineering works in Openshaw and the dwellers in colliery districts like Wigan and Atherton.'

This form of gambling is particularly obnoxious in that it is fraught with vital danger to one of the finest of our games, for it is to be feared that the methods which have led to the disrepute in which professional rowing and foot-racing on the flat are now held may utterly corrupt Association football also.

The means by which the coupons are distributed are in themselves remarkable, for in the greater number of cases the backer has no knowledge of his principal, who is quite usually a small bookmaker regularly following his calling during the ordinary racing season. The coupons are printed very cheaply by small local printers, and handed practically to anybody who will consent to act as agent. An agent is not hard to find, since he gets from one shilling and eightpence to two shillings in the pound for all bets received. He issues the forms wholesale; it may be in the great ironworks in which he is employed, or, if he be a carter, in the various cellars and warehouses of the firms upon whom he calls. Or sometimes he will take his stand at some particular street corner, there to issue the coupons and receive them back signed. They are not issued until the Thursday in each week, and the speculator hands the coupon with his stake to the agent not later than 2.30 P.M. on the Saturday. The bookmakers are usually honest men, and pay out the right amounts to those who win; but as they can offer only short odds for likely results, and more attractive odds only for more unlikely events, there are not many winners.

Apart altogether from other considerations, there can be no doubt that the manner in which nearly the whole of the inhabitants in many artisan districts confine their conversation from Thursday to Saturday night to football and its probable results must be injurious. Hardly ever during the conversation is the play itself so much talked of as is the likelihood of a man being able to win so much if he backs such and such teams. I am inclined to think that this constant practice of betting is doing not a little to affect the general steadiness of character amongst young workmen. A youth who has happened to win once or twice, or who feels certain, as so many do, that a week or two will see him the winner of a considerable sum, gradually becomes so obsessed that he loses the keen interest that he may have had in his work, and becomes indifferent to the risk of dismissal—dismissal which in many cases means absolute disaster to the home to which he belongs.[1]

Up against an evil of such magnitude as this canker of gambling and betting, the young worker among the poor may be pardoned if he feels a depressing sense of impotence. But he has no need to despair, for as a matter of fact he will have any number of at least indirect opportunities of fighting it. All that he does to bring into homes and lives from which all brightness has fled some realisation of the truth that life has in it what is infinitely finer than the acquisition of money, all that he does to promote rational recreation and healthy interests and to spread genuine education, all that he does to support and strengthen the idealism which even in the vilest districts may attempt to realise itself in the service of others—all this is work against gambling.

At the same time, though the individual can render valuable service to individuals, it must be admitted that no radical cure of the disease is likely to be effected without a vast change in the conditions of the people, a change which will mean a better adjustment of the relationship between wages and profits. Speaking broadly, the gambling fever is only one sign of the revolt of the people against underpaid labour in its many forms. It is useless to talk of the immorality of gambling and betting, and to blame men and women of the working classes who engage in it, without trying to

[1] For further information on this subject, see *Football Betting*, by Ainslie J. Robertson, M.A., a paper read before the Liverpool Economic and Statistical Society, 1907 ; and my article on ' The Football Fungus,' in *The Spectator* of March 12, 1913.

see something of their point of view. From the moral standpoint, incomparably worse is the evil wrought by the thoughtless example of people who indulge in such a habit when with all their advantages of birth and education they might be expected to find in life more worthy occupations and interests.

CHAPTER X

SETTLEMENTS AND GUILDS OF HELP

It is unnecessary at this date to explain what settlements are, or to repeat the oft-told tale of their origin. It will be familiar that the idea which they express is associated for all time with the names of F. D. Maurice, Edward Denison, Arnold Toynbee, and Canon Barnett; though possibly, as Sir Walter Besant has reminded us, it is in the writings of Carlyle that we must look for the first inspiration in the revival of the doctrine of personal service as the one thing needful.[1] But I feel it is of extreme importance that attention should be drawn to the position of the movement in the North of England, not only to the fact that settlements already exist, but to the great need that there is for work of this particular type.

For in the past, I think, relatively too much attention has been given to London. It was in London that the first settlements, Toynbee Hall in Whitechapel and Oxford House in Bethnal Green, sprang into being, both in the year 1885, and it is in these probably that the movement may still be seen at its best. Ten years passed before the two Manchester settlements were the first to be founded in the provinces, and similarly the first women's settlement, the Women's University

[1] Inaugural address, Mansfield House New Residence, 1897.

Settlement in Blackfriars, was started ten years before the Victoria Women's Settlement in Liverpool became in 1897 the first provincial place of the kind for female residents only. In 1898, the date of the publication of the still valuable book edited by the Rev. W. Reason on *University and Social Settlements*, there were some five-and-twenty settlements in London, but only six in the rest of England, and during the last fifteen years but little progress has been made. To this day appeals are constantly made to the men at Oxford and Cambridge to throw themselves into the work of the London settlements, as though there were no necessity for anything of the kind in other cities, and as though there were no other settlements actually in existence.

This tendency to focus youthful enthusiasm for social reform on one city to the practical exclusion of the rest is a serious misfortune for the country in general, and involves the loss of much possible good work. Large numbers of the men who go to the older Universities have their homes in the North, and the means which have enabled them to obtain their degrees have been acquired in the great industrial centres. Yet at Oxford and Cambridge they may hear constantly of the claims of London—claims which I do not for a moment wish to depreciate—but most probably will hear nothing of the social conditions of the northern cities. In some cases the claim on behalf of London fails to attract where a similar claim on behalf of familiar districts would find recognition. But when men are disposed to take up social work on leaving the University, the result of what they have heard is that they may go and work for a year or more in a

London settlement. Then on their return to the North in many cases they become absorbed in business and take no further interest, or only an academic interest, in settlement work. If such men, when they left the Universities, were attracted to settlements near to their own homes, it is more than probable that their impulse would endure; and that as they came to realise that the evil social surroundings of the people were actually the conditions of life of many of those in one way or another directly or indirectly concerned with the undertakings from which they obtained their wealth, they would be drawn to take not a fleeting but a permanent interest in the work, and probably in many cases would determine to play a part in the local government of their own particular locality. A surprising amount of energy and zeal is already being put into the work of the few northern settlements, but their usefulness might be enormously extended if a larger number of men and women were to come forward in support of the movement.

The first settlement to be founded in the North was the Manchester University Settlement in 1895, a ' mixed ' settlement started in connection with what was then Owen's College. A unique feature is its management of the Ancoats Art Museum, whose rooms are used for settlement purposes, and on the premises of which the women residents actually reside. Among its many activities may be mentioned Lectures on Art, Debating Societies, ' At Homes,' Dances, Smoking Concerts, Poor Man's Lawyer (consulted by about two thousand persons *per annum*), Little Girls' Club, and work on behalf of cripples, including the school already mentioned in Chapter IV. This is a settle-

ment which does excellent work and offers bound-
less opportunities to the keen worker, for the number
of residents is far from adequate to the needs of
the district.   The Lancashire College Settlement
was founded in the same year by the Congregational
body.   It is situated in Hulme, which I have
already referred to as the poorest and most neglected
area of Manchester.   Unfortunately, owing to lack
of support, it came to an end in 1912, but an attempt
is being made to replace it by a new undenomina-
tional settlement.

The Victoria Settlement in Liverpool can accom-
modate no more than eight resident ladies, but they
are assisted by large numbers of outside workers.
Like the Manchester University Settlement it is
crippled for want of sufficient income.   The Liverpool University Settlement, started in 1896, extended its premises in 1908, and has recently been
enlarged and rebuilt.   It provides employment
for numerous associates besides its residents, and is
a very flourishing institution.

The Croft House Settlement at Sheffield, which
takes as its motto Lord Acton's phrase, ' The
redemption of Poverty is not in the material resources of the rich, but in the moral resources of
the poor,' is in its twelfth year.   Its Vacation
School and Guild of Play for children, and its clubs
for men, boys, and girls, and allied activities are the
most conspicuous feature of its work.   It is well
supported, but with more money and more workers
could extend its usefulness.

In Leeds a small women's settlement—the Red
House—has just been started, but there is no place
of the kind for men among all its 446,000 inhabitants.   A worker in the city points to this as perhaps

its first practical need, for, he says, ' there are districts in Leeds which are more lost than the worst quarters of London. There are miles of mean streets in which ignorance and child deformity are almost normal : there are districts in which the depth of moral depravity cannot be named. There is an absence of beauty which is terrible. And yet the people are not an unlovable people. They have many of the defects of strength and independence as well as the faults of weakness. But they have great qualities and a high level of intelligence obscured by the all-pervading spirit of distrust and materialism.'

With the above my list of northern settlements is complete. There may be others ; I do not know them. The number is pitiably small ; the support given to these few equally pitiable. It is indeed matter for amazement that an idea potentially pregnant, I am bold to say, with every whit as much social good as the idea, say, which inspired the Boy Scout movement should have had comparatively so little result. But settlement life has been little advertised ; it is not showy or picturesque ; it means, in the little-known provincial settlements at any rate, real self-sacrifice—the foregoing of the ordinary social pleasures of the well-to-do to spend oneself upon persons who appear utterly unattractive, sordid, irremediable in their squalor of body and soul—a thankless task at first sight.

But uphill work as it may seem, the essential feature of all settlement activity, namely, that men and women who have enjoyed a refined upbringing should deliberately go and live among working people, is probably the most effective way in which a real sense of class brotherhood may be developed. The poor, becoming actually acquainted with the manner of life of the settlers, learn to place in them a confidence rarely gained by the worker who comes for a certain number of hours from an unknown suburban paradise. For an obvious advantage among many involved in the existence of settlements in the poorest districts is the fact that the resident is nearly always available, no matter what the hour of the night, and is not fettered and hindered in all that he does by the knowledge that a train or a tram-car has to be caught to take him back to his home. Much of the finest work in connection with any settlement will consist in visiting at times of trouble and distress of all kinds the people in whom the settler has become interested, and who in their turn feel that he or she may be regarded and depended on as a friend. Stress is often laid by advocates of the life on its value as a means to research and investigation into social conditions, but quite apart from and beyond this lies the supreme value of human sympathy, without which the settlement is in my opinion of small worth indeed.

Occasionally there are instances in which settlers have not this sympathy. They may look upon a year or two in the slums as a useful preparation for a literary or political career, or they may be merely concerned in producing tables of statistics and compiling what is called ' information '—usually in support of some callow theory—respecting the conditions of family life of certain types of the population. I, for one, question very much the value of work of this particular kind, for long experience has taught me that the mere curious inquirer who has no sympathetic interest in the people, no feelings of actual friendliness with those with whom he comes in contact, will not arrive at the truth, but often only obtain the answers he desires to the very leading questions which he puts. The utterly ridiculous reports based on investigations of this kind that are sometimes issued are a nightmare to those who actually know the conditions of the labourer's life, and appreciate how much harm may be done by persons who regard the poor not as brothers in Christ but as so much interesting material for study. Settlement work at its best is a very different thing, and undoubtedly provides one of the most practical and natural means of approaching many of the social problems with which the country is confronted. Granted that the settler's aim is in the first place to love not to learn, to give not to gain, it affords unequalled opportunities for the obtaining of first-hand knowledge, and gives facilities for an intercourse with the workers which cannot be obtained in other ways. The settlement formed of settlers of the right type —educated men or women of infinite patience and tolerance, not without humour, largely endowed with the optimism of a living faith and inspired by unerring singleness of heart—must in whatever district it exists become a centre of much that will raise the social and religious ideals of the people.

For those who for any reason are unable to devote themselves to settlement work, the organisations called Guilds or Leagues of Help which have sprung up in recent years may provide an excellent outlet for energy on behalf of their fellows, and one available for him who has but an hour or two in the week for social work no less than for a ' whole-timer.' These guilds are founded more or less on the model of the well-known Elberfeld System, which may be briefly described as one which provides in every poor city district a helper or friend for a certain number of families. He or she engages to take an active personal interest in their members, and in time of trouble or unemployment will exert himself to find means of extricating them from their difficulties. Such a society commonly has a head for each small district, and the various heads usually meet together under the control of a divisional chairman. The divisional chairmen in their turn form an executive committee for the organisation, covering the whole town in which it has been set up.

The guilds are not in any way charitable bodies. It is not their function to administer relief, but rather to give friendship to those who need it; to put families or persons in touch with the right society or body to help a particular need; to promote co-operation between societies and institutions engaged in the same kind of work, and by means of statistical information to obtain definite data upon which plans for reform may be based. Wherever they have come into existence—and it is noteworthy that of the fifty affiliated to the National Association of Guilds of Help thirty-two are in the North—they have done much to prevent that overlapping of charity which is one of the most fruitful causes of continued poverty. Here is an opportunity for the man or woman who does not feel particularly fitted for work among young people, but who yet is filled with an ardent desire to do something to benefit the community. There is no Guild of Help which is not in need of further assistance, and the field of service open to the activities of any one who may feel inclined to take a share in such efforts is very wide indeed.

I

Bolton, Bradford, Eccles, Halifax, Huddersfield, Hull, Manchester, Middlesboro', Newcastle, Oldham, Sunderland, Warrington, and other towns have exceedingly active organisations of the kind, while Liverpool has set up (November 1909) a ' Council of Voluntary Aid,' which should prove of enormous value to the city, if the workers equal the organisation. ' It is a council representative of all the forms of charitable and social effort in the city, and of the elected and official members of the local public bodies. It may be said to be a general body providing facilities for co-operation between the various voluntary social agencies of the city, and for bringing them into systematic relation with official agencies.' The whole Council meets but once a year, but it is divided into six group committees, dealing with (1) Medical Charities, (2) Institutions for the Aged and Afflicted, (3) Relief in the Homes of the Poor, (4) Children's Institutions and Homes, (5) Reformatory Agencies, (6) Social Improvement and Education. These meet once a quarter, or oftener as occasion may require, and when expedient summon conferences. There are also an executive committee meeting monthly and various special and sub-committees. Work is carried on in close co-operation with the Charity Organisation Society, which acts as the executive agent of the Council. Numerous reports and leaflets on such subjects as Rescue Work, Infant Care, Children's Holidays, the Treatment of Phthisis, etc., have already been published. Reports of local institutions, press-cuttings, and blue-books are collected and filed, and the offices of the Council form a bureau of information and advice for social workers of every kind.

The Manchester City League of Help, founded in 1906, has very similar aims, specifying its objects as, ' To unite citizens of all classes, both men and women, irrespective of religious or political opinions, for the following purposes :

(a) To provide a friend for those in need of help or advice.

(b) To deepen the sense of civic responsibility for the care of the poor.

(c) To promote co-operation among public and charitable agencies and social workers in the city.'

Its Committees correspond not with spheres of work, but with fifteen districts of the city. The fact that the number of voluntary workers increased from 650 in October 1912 to 766 in October 1913 is a sign of its vigorous life, which is devoted to the endeavour to be a general clearing-house for the operations of all charitable agencies, and to act in co-operation with the Boards of Guardians, Labour Exchange, Sanitary, Education, and Pensions Committees. An analysis, made for the first time last year, of the causes of distress in the families whose cases were brought to the notice of the League yielded most interesting results. They were as follows :

Sickness	1243
Widowhood . . .	180
Unemployment . . .	357
Accident	120
Old Age	162
Character, Drink, etc. . .	255
Desertion and Maintenance Order	52
Unclassified	184

Such figures should serve to refute the argument of the mean and hard-hearted persons who refuse to contribute to charities on the ground that the calamities of the poor are nearly always all their own fault. An excellent handbook, comprising a complete list of the public and charitable institutions of Manchester, is issued for the use of helpers. Similar booklets are published, among others, by the Bradford City Guild of Help, founded in 1904, by the Newcastle Citizens' Guild of Help, founded in 1909, and by the Bolton Guild of Help, founded in 1905. This latter, in addition to its more general work, has specially concerned itself with warfare on consumption. It has also undertaken the supervision of the youths discharged locally from Borstal Institutions. A Mutual Registry of Assistance, now controlled by a separate committee, owes its existence to the Guild. All public and charitable bodies are invited to supply details of persons assisted, and thus waste and overlapping are averted and more efficient aid is available for the necessitous. Four thousand seven hundred and twenty-two families were registered during 1912, the first year of the work of the organisation.

In these Guilds of Help we have a movement which is making a not unsuccessful attempt to grapple with some of the social problems of our day. Yet it again is crippled for want of suitable helpers, and for want of them time after time is compelled to accept the services of persons who, however willing, have not the knowledge and general width of outlook which are imperatively needed if the questions they are continually being called upon to face are to be effectively dealt with.

But a spirit of indifference is abroad which causes men, and women too, when the subject of religion is named, to shrug their shoulders as though it were one with nothing in it of the least interest to themselves.

Now while I am certain that the origin of this lamentable indifference is far too deep-seated for me to attempt to locate ; whilst I am certain that the remedy can only be found in the spiritual, not in the material, sphere ; whilst I believe that what is most wanting and most needed is holiness and ever more holiness in the clergy, a still loftier vision of the Divine Goodness, which shall find expression in their lives in that manifest ' beauty of holiness ' which is the greatest soul-compelling force in the world—while these are my convictions, I cannot agree with those who say that because for the minister of religion the spiritual welfare of the people is everything, it is no part of his duty to attempt to interfere with social conditions. For when he sees, as see he must, that in case after case the spiritual welfare he is concerned about is hindered or choked by the growth of gambling or drinking habits, by the wretched conditions under which so many have to live, by the cruel pressure of sweated industries, how should he not strive to destroy these tares which cover his field ? The people still need to be convinced that the clergy are not merely concerned with filling their churches, but care for them as real friends always care, *i.e.* for body and soul as one entity. Therefore I believe that an active, concerted crusade by the various denominations against material evils would enormously strengthen their spiritual influence. A deep religious spirit exists in the heart of the people.

From time to time, during periods of distress and trouble, this is evidenced even among the apparently most irreligious, and it is always ready to be called into activity if the call be made in a way to which the soul can respond.

I myself feel—it is a purely personal view—that where the educated man seeks to spend something of the forces of sympathy and kindness which he has at his disposal among those who are less fortunate, with a quite obvious disregard for all the influences of religion, he may do quite as much harm as good. No mere code of morality will provide for the dweller in a slum area anything like the inspiration of religion, or give that elevation to life which alone makes it of value to the individual. While therefore I welcome whatever may be done on behalf of the people, I feel that what is most essential is that it should be recognised by those among whom the social worker's lot is cast that it is the love of God which has prompted him to do the work to which he has set his hand. Social work which in any way weakens the hold of religion seems to me deplorable.

In my own experience, with rare exceptions, the clergy are in their various parishes the leaders in all that goes to promote the general uplifting of the people. But they are usually overburdened with care and anxiety. Were their resources, either in men or in money, at all commensurate with their aspirations and needs, they would be an infinitely greater factor in the amelioration of social conditions.

The value of the work of the clergy in poor parishes must not be measured by the attendance at church. That may be far from what it ought to be, but it must not be forgotten that a man who may be the constant friend and helper of the poor may be anything but a good preacher, whilst eloquence in the pulpit is not always associated with devotion to the poorest parishioners. In not a few cases the crowded church is filled not with parishioners, but with persons who from all directions will flock to hear the words of a really eloquent man.

The position of the clergy in many of the poorer parts of our northern towns is a very difficult one. Very often they have to work single-handed or with one colleague, among a teeming, shifting population of the very poor. They are often, alas, harassed by poverty and ill-health in their own homes. Besides the direct work of their ministry they have to be responsible for the working of social agencies which make for the betterment of the condition of the people. They have personally to superintend and conduct clubs and brigades for the young people, to organise entertainments, raise money for special purposes, and to bear the chief responsibility of their church and parochial finances. Much of this work—work which undoubtedly often absorbs so much of the time and energy of the clergy that it clogs their mental and spiritual activities—ought to be done by laymen, but in these poor town parishes there are no laymen to do it.

There are districts in Manchester, and indeed in all our northern towns, where the only people of education and culture living amongst the people are the clergymen of various denominations and a few medical practitioners. Their work is often peculiarly disheartening, peculiarly likely to in-

duce 'staleness' in any but the stoutest souls. To
make any discernible impression in a very poor
district is extraordinarily difficult. And when
people *are* persuaded to live a new life, instead of
becoming a strength to their church, one of their
first impulses is to migrate from the slum parish
to a more respectable district. Those unthinking
persons who censure the apparent failure of the
churches to touch great masses of the population
may be admonished that the failure, if failure it
be, lies not a little at the door of the educated layman, who might, if he would, do very much to
improve matters. How often we hear people
grumble ' The Church ought to do more,' ' The
Church ought to do so and so,' and all the time
they think of the *clergy* as the *Church*, and forget
that they themselves are the Church, and that out
of their own mouths they are condemned. In
many directions there are none who can render
more effective service than those who are fresh
from school or university, and unencumbered with
household cares of any kind. Here surely lies an
opportunity for men of good will to come to the
assistance of the Church. If they will only throw
themselves into the work, they can accomplish
much in raising the whole tone and moral character
of a poor parish.

It is often said, and not infrequently, I fear, said
with truth, that parochial clergymen are difficult
to work with, and want to control everything themselves, and leave no field for the layman. But
the statement is sometimes made merely as an
excuse for doing nothing at all, and there are
countless parishes where men would be received
with open arms, and be given every possible scope

for work among the people in the name of the Church.

Again, it has become, I am told, almost 'the thing' on the part of a portion of the religious press, and—it is with diffidence I repeat it—especially on the part of clergy who live in communities, to disparage more or less what is called 'the resident gentleman in the parish.' But nobody who has had the actual experience of such a life lived in contact with the clergy can be wanting in appreciation of it. The vicars of our poor northern parishes will warmly welcome the aid of educated laymen who will settle within their bounds and co-operate with them on behalf of their people. No finer work can be undertaken. It abounds in opportunities for effective service for God and man.

I do not forget the assistance which the Guilds of Help may be to the clergy of poor parishes; but this movement, like others, needs for its helpers persons of rare tact and sympathy, and these are not always to be found. Even where Guilds of Help have been established, the clergyman still very frequently remains the one real friend of the poor.

It is well not to overlook the fact that through recent changes in our educational system the clergy in many districts have been deprived of the services of a man who was formerly one of their chief helpers. I refer to that much misunderstood and much misrepresented individual, the Church schoolmaster. He usually lived among the people; he knew them well; he voluntarily and wholeheartedly threw himself into the social work of the district. Now that the schools are under the control of the municipal authorities, too often the schoolmaster, like the better-class tradesman of the district, lives in the suburbs, and only comes into the parish for his scholastic duties.

I venture to doubt whether the work of any communities of clergy living together, or of Sisters of Mercy, or of ladies coming in from outside to help in poor districts, will ever equal in value that accomplished by a devoted pastor and his wife. Celibates and visitors from a distance rarely gain that intimate knowledge, and more particularly that confidence of the people, which is given to the best kind of clergyman's wife. And for the rest the best work, I believe, may be done from settlements, whether of men or women, sympathising and cooperating with the various religious bodies. For the great desideratum is that social workers should live amongst the people.

On one criticism I must venture. In many districts there is, I think, a certain lack of sympathy on the part of the clergy with various organisations for young people and others which are not directly connected with the Church. But the fault is not altogether on one side, and non-denominational workers might well make more effort to invite the interest of the clergy instead of leaving them to infer that they prefer to be left alone. One of the problems of the time, which an influx of educated men into poor districts might serve to solve, would be the linking-up so far as is possible of the various organisations working for good, so that the Church—I use the word in its very widest sense—may be united in its attack upon all that is evil in the social conditions of the day, and in its effort to make Christianity not merely a name but the dominating force in every quarter of our cities.

CHAPTER XII

THE social problems of Newcastle-upon-Tyne and the district arise in the main from the same root causes which operate in other large English towns, modified in certain directions by climatic and industrial conditions.

The city, whose origin dates back to Hadrian, has been aptly called 'The Metropolis of the North'; and, though a town of only 270,000 inhabitants, has great significance in all directions over a considerable area. It is the principal commercial city in the area between a line drawn from east to west immediately south of Glasgow, and a parallel line drawn just north of Leeds; and with Gateshead on the opposite side of the river, and contingent riverside towns, has a total population not far short of three quarters of a million.

In the main its citizens owe their prosperity to its position in the coal-fields and on the banks of a very useful river. Its capacity for shipbuilding, boilermaking, engineering, and foundry work are

---

[1] I have only edited this chapter, which is the work of Mr. Henry B. Saint, hon. secretary of the local Guild of Help. It seemed well to me, after the method followed in previous chapters, to endeavour to present as it were a bird's-eye view of the social life and problems of one city as a separate whole.

all determined mainly by the river and the adjacent coal supply.

The shipbuilding and engineering works, founded by the late Lord Armstrong, employ in busy times some 26,000 workpeople. Shipbuilding yards such as Swan, Hunter, and Wigham Richardson's, which produced the *Mauretania*, and Palmer's, which are entrusted from time to time with the building of warships, are indications of the importance of the city. Last year (1912) ships to the total of 397,000 tons were built on the Tyne, this being the largest output, after that of the Clyde, of any river in the United Kingdom. When business is good the shipbuilding and engineering works on the Tyne employ between 40,000 and 50,000 men.

The northern coal-field covers a very large area of the eastern portions of Northumberland and Durham. It is a spearhead-shaped tract running from Amble in Northumberland to Auckland in Durham, and measures 800 square miles. The produce is mainly shipped by way of the Tyne, although considerable tonnage is now finding its outlet at the neighbouring port of Blyth, some ten miles from the mouth of the river. Last year the coal production of Northumberland was 13,381,641 tons, and that of Durham 37,890,404 tons.

The river Tyne provides occupation for merchants dealing in many kinds of wares, which are forwarded to all parts of the earth by what, assembled together, would form a very large fleet of vessels. In 1911 nearly 6,000,000 tons of merchandise were entered inwards and nearly 7,000,000 tons cleared outwards, placing the Tyne in the third and fourth positions respectively in the United Kingdom. The traffic of a port so large us this necessarily involves a great amount of dock and transit labour, and of course much casual labour.

It is impossible to deal with social matters concerning the Newcastle district without giving a definite place to the coal-miners, who form a very considerable proportion of the population of Northumberland and Durham. The number of workers connected with the collieries in these two counties may be put at 60,000 and 160,000 respectively.

The work of the hewers is done in ' shifts.' There are three shifts worked in practically the whole of Durham, but only a quarter of Northumberland is worked in this manner. A shift involves seven to seven and a half hours' work from bank to bank. On an average the men work five shifts in one week.

It is hardly possible to make a general statement regarding wages, as there is variation in different areas and different collieries, and the result partly depends upon the nature of the coal which the collier has to hew. Payment is made on tonnage. As a general statement it may be said that the earnings in Northumberland are about £2 per week, and in Durham a little less. ' Putters ' of sixteen to twenty-one years of age, who work on ' piece,' make 5s. to 7s. per day, but most of the men who are not hewing coal are paid on a basis of time, and not per ton. The majority of married men, in addition to wages, have a free house and free coal, which together may be taken as equivalent to 5s. per week.

A considerable amount of time is lost by the men. At one colliery it is estimated that twenty per cent. of time is regularly lost, but this is quite exceptional, the average loss being about ten per cent. When fortnightly 'pays' were the rule, the Mondays which followed the pay Saturdays were slack days to the disadvantage of both master and workman. 'Pays' in Northumberland are now generally weekly instead of fortnightly, but the results can hardly be determined as yet.

Drinking is a common vice. Without doubt the workmen's clubs which have sprung up in a great number of colliery districts have had a deleterious effect. But the colliers of Northumberland are a good class of men, and until recently were an almost distinct order, free from intermixture from other parts of England. They show much intelligence, and their interest in, and powers of, study have been very marked in many instances. They contribute a considerable number of local preachers to the Methodist body, and are very often men of forceful character. The Right Honourable Thomas Burt, P.C., for some time past 'father' of the House of Commons, was a working collier, as was his fellow member for a neighbouring division, Charles Fenwick. Both are men most highly respected in and outside the House.

Nearly every colliery village has its institute, containing a reading-room and library. Billiards and other games are often provided, but gambling is strictly forbidden. The colliers are fond of sports such as football, quoits, running, and bowls, and hardly a house is without one or more bicycles. Again, an American organ or piano is generally found in the collier's cottage, and music is much enjoyed. The people are cleanly in habit, and healthy, and many are well housed, although some of the older dwellings might well be replaced by modern buildings. As a class the colliery folk may be described as religious. Scarcely a child can be found who does not attend Sunday School.

The city of Newcastle is healthily and pleasantly placed on the hilly north bank of the Tyne some ten miles from its mouth, and is, on the whole, well laid out. It is attractive architecturally in its main thoroughfares, and particularly in the lower parts of the city recalls ancient times with its seventeenth-century overhanging houses, and their many small windows. These, however, are rapidly being replaced by modern buildings without romance and less picturesque. The old Norman Keep, known as the Castle, the Cathedral, with its unusual and very beautiful ' glory crown of spires,' and the remains of the city walls and gates have a fascination for the antiquarian and the imaginative.

The citizens possess an uncommon privilege in the Town Moor, which together with the adjoining grass-land, The Leazes, gives them some thousand acres in perpetuity for their games, walking, riding, and golf. The parks (one of great beauty) and recreation grounds furnish 284 acres more. The city has an excellent service of electric trains running close to many of the factory areas on the river, on to the coast, and back again by a more interior route. Near the mouth of the Tyne are situated four attractive seaside resorts on a coastline beautiful by reason of its sands and rocks, and very valuable in its influence on the health and enjoyment of the working population of the district.

The climate is for the hardy and strenuous. In winter and spring keen winds blow from the northeast and east, testing the weak-chested and delicate. To the healthy they are stimulating, and no doubt the bracing air of the north-east accounts for much

of the sturdiness of the men of the district. Probably the climatic rigours are among the causes of
the high drinking statistics to be noted presently.

If one were to arrive at Newcastle as a stranger,
and use one's observation intelligently for a period
of some months, the broad impression gained would
be that of a comely city, inhabited by a prosperous,
self-reliant community, given to sociability, and
greatly to sport and amusement, with some liking
for intellectual pursuits, not largely gifted with
artistic perception, and as a whole, whilst showing
some public spirit in the use of wealth, of defective
civic sense. Much money is earned, but not enough
is spent. A close investigation would reveal the
usual distressing factors of our large industrial
cities.

The present writer suffered considerable humilia-
tion some years ago in presence of a Norwegian
boy on his way to an English school and temporarily
under his charge. The youth was arrested by a
sight very common in the streets of Newcastle—a
barefooted, ragged urchin—and stood with wide-
open eyes in an attitude of amazement, uttering
words expressive of the utmost surprise. In the
richest country of Europe he was shocked by this
spectacle not to be found in his own, which is
probably the poorest. It is significant that the
incident should have happened in one of the hand-
somest thoroughfares of the city, in which are
situated four important banks, several insurance
companies' offices, the Cathedral, the Town Hall,
and offices of the Corporation—symbols of wealth,
prudence, religion, and civic oversight. In the
midst of every influence which ought at least
to produce cleanliness and cover nakedness, this

K

neglected child stood as a rebuke to the signs of apparent prosperity everywhere around.

It is disturbing to read that, among other obstacles encountered by our medical inspectors of schools, ' The conditions of living of most of the poor are such that cleanliness of body and clothing is not easy to maintain.'

No nation and no city which openly and without shame display such a condition of affairs can claim to have reached a high level of patriotism and civic elevation. The fact is that our large cities exhibit almost as much inconsistency as the human mind itself—a mixture of wretchedness and happiness, of poverty and wealth, of thrift and wastefulness, of hard work and sloth—which is another way of saying that they consist of the children of men, and that Newcastle is no exception to the rule. The healing word is *character* expressed in citizenship.

In any attempt to indicate some of the social factors which make up the total which we call Newcastle and district, it is desirable to remember that problems are created, not merely by lack of money, but by wrong ways of spending, and that the adjustments which are necessary to produce the ideal citizen must affect both extremes and all degrees between. The social problem is not simply one of the poor but also of the rich—indeed of all classes. It is true that such buildings as the Armstrong College, which owes its existence largely to the generosity of the men of the North, and the Royal Victoria Infirmary, for which the city is indebted to the munificent donations of two of its prominent citizens and the smaller donations of a great number of obscure Northumbrians, and the

Laing Art Gallery and a number of the smaller Free Libraries, and many other evidences of the thoughtfulness and generosity of its citizens are signs that Newcastle is not entirely without sympathy for common needs. On the other hand much more could be done. Considerable slum areas and much preventable poverty furnish serious drawbacks to city life and temper. It is contended that the fundamental evil is that some at any rate of the working classes are underpaid. This is no doubt a fact, but the problem is not so simple a one as it appears, since Newcastle cannot do otherwise than suffer under the competitive system which rules the rest of the world. It is urged by employers that higher wages in certain trades are impossible. But the results which have followed an increase in wages have shown that improvement can be effected in some cases without serious dislocation. It is evident that whilst there is what looks like, or actually is, unfair remuneration industrial unrest will continue. Still we must remember that payment of higher wages, which are certainly due in many cases, even were they to amount to double the present rate, would not by itself necessarily produce better men and women or better citizens. There would certainly be improved health and increased facilities for obtaining the desirable amenities of life which are commonly denied to the poor. But the supreme consideration is after all, as I have said before, the production of character. Higher rates of wages ought to be paid, and eventually will be paid where due—but after that ? Will all be well then ? As a matter of fact some of the factory workers on piecework at special jobs earn the salary of a member of Parliament, and more. And it is impossible to assume that these social questions only involve one class of the community.

Wages in Newcastle, speaking generally, compare favourably with those obtaining in most industrial centres. The following, which apply to the main bodies of workers apart from colliers, who have already been referred to, are instances :

The general labourer in the engineering works makes from 21s. to 23s. a week, and where a certain amount of skill is involved, up to 31s. Trained men such as fitters, turners, and blacksmiths make 37s. a week. To these figures may be added, when trade is brisk, ten per cent. earned by overtime and night-work.

In the shipbuilding yards the wages are practically the same, but some men on piecework earn special wages, as for instance the average plater who makes 22s. 6d. to 30s. per *day*, and the riveter who makes per *day* 22s. to 25s. Boilermakers on ' piece ' earn £3 to £5 per week ; on ' time ' £2.

Employers complain of the amount of time lost. In the shipyards it is considerable ; in fact, in certain cases there is a loss from weather and other causes estimated at twenty-five to thirty-five per cent. Some men in well-paid positions can earn as much as they need by working four or five days a week. Others whose occupation is particularly arduous work only three or four days a week, and apparently with good reason. But the lower grades of workmen depending upon them suffer, and where the absences cannot be calculated the employer is much inconvenienced. But the working-man as a rule keeps good time. The standard hours are fifty-three in engineering and fifty-four in shipbuilding.

The conditions under which the men work must be described as, on the whole, good. Where there are dangerous trades, such as the lead industry, employers furnish the means of avoiding contamination, though not always with success, as some of the workpeople find the precautions irksome.

The extreme north is not an area in which the woman worker is in great request, differing in that respect from the Lancashire districts where she is so important a factor.   In Newcastle a local pottery, a rabbit-down factory, and departments in one of the large engineering works employ a fair number of women; and there are, of course, the usual women's occupations, such as typewriting, in connection with business establishments. These do not call for special attention. It should be noted, however, that increasing opportunities are offered to girls of fair intelligence in offices and by business firms, and that to some extent girls are displacing the ordinary male clerk. Some firms pay highly for skilled typists, but, on the other hand, a considerable number of girls work for about 10s. per week.

Rents are undoubtedly high in Newcastle. This is partly because the growth of the city is restricted on the north by the large Town Moor area and on the south by the river, and is partly due to the rates of wages and to good employment. Land and building costs are both heavy. Nevertheless the building trade until the last few years has been a very busy one, and great expansion has taken place on the outskirts, where two to four-roomed flats (two-storied houses) and self-contained houses of five to seven rooms have been provided in abundance. Rentals within the city are roughly as follows :

> One room, 1s. to 3s. 9d., according to size and situation of room.
>
> Two rooms, 2s. 6d. to 5s. 6d., according to size and situation of room.
>
> Three rooms, 4s. to 7s. 9d., according to situation and accommodation, also the higher rent generally includes scullery and bath.
>
> Four rooms, 5s. 3d. to 9s. The lower figure applies to a block of property in the east end of the city let at an exceptionally low rent.
>
> Five and six rooms, 10s. 6d. to 12s. 6d. Good class flats.
>
> Five and six rooms, £18 to £32, and rates. Self-contained.

The popular shops which lie on the three main routes, not a mile in length altogether, bring in extraordinary rents, said in some cases to be as large as those in New Bond Street, London.

The drink problem is important, though the casual visitor in walking through the streets of Newcastle would not regard the evidences of drinking as very alarming. Statistics during the last thirty years show a falling off in the number of convictions for drunkenness from 4245 in 1882 to 2708 in 1912. But Newcastle stands, for the year 1911, the seventh most drunken amongst sixty-six towns of England and Wales, the convictions amounting to 97.91 per 10,000 of the population. This is far exceeded by Middlesbrough with 111.75, and Liverpool with 152.93 per 10,000 inhabitants. Newcastle has one public-house to every 112 families, or if 'on' and 'off' licences are reckoned

together, one licence to every 86 families. (The
Royal Commission on Liquor Licensing Law
(1899) advises one to each 750.) Its drink bill
for 1912 was £990,500. The county of Northumberland is of all the English counties by far the
most drunken, showing for the year 1911 127.31
convictions per 10,000 of the population. Durham with 65.93 shows the next worst figures,
whilst Oxford has the lowest, namely, 6.50. Statistics are, of course, proverbially misleading, and
considerable allowance must be made for such
factors as rigid supervision, etc. But these figures
are serious. Not only does the habit tend to produce crime and poverty, but it has a terrible effect
upon the rising generation and its education, and
upon the industries of the district, where it causes
much interruption, to the detriment of the delin-
quents themselves and of their employers. It
must be said, however, that in spite of drunkenness
the statistics of crime are not specially alarming,
whilst those relating to serious crime are steadily
improving. The statistics of crime for this district
in 1912 were the lowest for over twenty years,
though throughout the country generally there had
been an increase. But as regards pauperism Newcastle does not compare well with other English
cities of its size.

The housing problem is a serious one. There
are 10,412 persons occupying single rooms with an
average of 4.2 persons per room. The regulations
as to cubic feet of air are not easy to maintain, as
even where rooms are let on the condition that
only the stipulated number of persons shall inhabit
them, evasions take place by the introduction of
further persons later, and the process of enforcing

obedience by ejection is not in practice an easy one.   There are 81,118 persons in the city occupying their dwellings at a rate exceeding two persons to a room.   The law makes no regulation as to separation of the sexes in a room used for sleeping. It allows a room to be used by an unlimited number of persons for living and sleeping in, so long as there are 400 cubic feet of space for each adult and 200 for each child.   The City Corporation has provided a number of dwellings of one or more rooms which are very useful, but only to a small degree meet the needs of the case.   For the most part they involve an annual loss.   A corporation cannot build so cheaply as a private builder.   It is very questionable on several grounds whether the city ought to provide for housing at a loss.

In spite of bad housing the health of the city is on the whole good, as may be gauged by the fact that the birth-rate for 1912 was 26.8 per thousand of the population, and the death-rate 14.3 (a record for Newcastle), whilst infant mortality was 101 per 1000 births.   But 1912, owing to the absence of heat, was favourable to infantile health.   The neighbouring town of Gateshead shows nearly as good figures.   The health of the community is in excellent hands so far as the City Health officials can affect it.   The Midwives and Notification of Births Acts have been of marked benefit.   There is a Superintendent of Midwives and a Mothers' and Babies' Welcome Society.   The city possesses eight swimming and general baths, one Turkish bath, and five washhouses.

A very energetic and capable Education Committee controls the teaching in fifty-four Ele-

mentary Schools, including two for the feeble-
minded, and has liberal views in the matter of
providing meals for children. A Juvenile Advisory
Committee has just been established under its
auspices. Medical inspection of the whole of the
Committee's schools is carried out in a very capable
manner by a chief inspector with two whole-time
assistants, two nurses, and two clerks. There is a
hope that before long open-air classes and schools
may be established as in some other cities.

The Workers' Education Association has considerable hold in Newcastle and does excellent work.
Some of the religious bodies, and notably the
Y.M.C.A. and Y.W.C.A., hold educative classes
on various subjects. All these agencies must be
remembered as against the immense amount of
attention which is given to amusements and sports,
not any of them in themselves harmful, but only
as they are abused. It certainly, however, is a
matter for serious debate whether the general intelligence of the community is not losing in depth.
There does not seem to be the same amount of
serious search for knowledge and the close study
that prevailed a generation ago. It is difficult to
make a positive affirmation on this point, but the
impression given to many is that just stated.

Some sixty or seventy medical and other charities
administer relief and comfort to great numbers.
Children are especially well looked after. A movement is on foot to promote co-ordination so that
overlapping may be prevented and joint action for
public welfare made possible. There is an active
Guild of Help which, by means of two hundred
and fifty voluntary helpers, endeavours to provide sympathetic assistance for persons in distress.

There is also an excellent Charity Organisation Society.

Of religious accommodation for the population there is no lack. The attendances at church, chapel, and mission-room are good in some parishes and poor in others. The Brotherhood movement flourishes. In Newcastle and district there are 48 men's (8000 members) and 16 women's (1500 members) meetings. And there are in the district 13 men's and 8 women's Adult Schools, with a membership of 506 men and 637 women. This form of meeting is very promising. It is held at the unpopular hour of 9 A.M. on Sundays, and differs from the Brotherhood meetings in that it consists of much smaller groups, ranging from ten persons upwards, in exceptional cases rising to a hundred. In no instance is the audience too large to admit of free, frank discussion, which ranges over various fields of knowledge, and is often remarkably candid and stimulating. Admirable programmes are arranged in sequence, so that a definite, ordered advance in knowledge is made. A handbook is published with notes on the subjects studied.

This in brief is the material Newcastle offers for discussion of the problems of social welfare. When one comes to consider solutions one realises that there must be, not one, but many. Very great things are being done, and can be done, and will be done on the line of economics. But it is obvious that no permanent and vital improvement can be made if sight is lost of the fact that the whole community must share responsibility and come under survey. It is the individual will that must be influenced. The preservation of self-respect and the fostering of initiative are priceless. It is useless to set up housing schemes, for instance, without realising at the same time that the attitude of the occupiers towards order and cleanliness must be sound. Neither can the wealthy hope to produce a noble city by the mere giving of sums of money for doles or for the building of institutions. There must come from that side a contribution of sympathy and fellow-feeling, exhibiting itself in the just apportionment of earnings, the provision of healthy workshops, and the arrangement of proper hours of labour—unmistakable indications in fact that the employer regards the employee as a fellow-citizen, a contributor to the general prosperity, including his own, and a gauge by which the character of the city and nation will be estimated. There are schools for the inculcation of methods of money-making. Where are the schools teaching the equally important, if not more important, art, and wisdom, and need of money-spending ? The whole popular attitude towards money needs revision. We must come to see as an actual article of faith not only that we live *by* one another, but that to a very definite degree we must live *for* one another. From appreciation of this truth would arise such an adjustment of industrial circumstances as would largely take the sting away from present problems. It is very necessary that there should be fostered by private and public speech and written word, by every means available, a civic spirit, which should endeavour to teach children from their earliest years to take an interest in their city and the State, to understand them, and work in their service. How much more effective would be such a frame of mind on both sides than can be legal enactments! Let us hope that ere long a man will more commonly realise that he himself and men generally and as individuals, men of all classes, must do justly, think kindly, and make an atmosphere in which eventually wrong will decline and right thrive. He will give the best chance possible to others while seeking reasonable openings himself.

It is obvious to the thoughtful that schemes which are not in the last resort built upon character cannot succeed. The education of the youth of the city is a profitable field of operations, and offers plastic material to the wise teacher. If we try we can succeed in bringing into our schools a system of education which will not merely insert facts, but produce in the scholar a taste for learning and an attitude towards his fellow-scholars which may be indicated by the popular phrase ' playing the game.' Our education must train the mind to educate itself, must inculcate a right moral attitude towards the difficulties and the tasks of life, and a standard of honour which will be serviceable to the city and State, and raise its possessor above many misdeeds. This kind of education demands teachers with the highest possible qualifications, and greatly increased expenditure, which however would inevitably be cheap in the end. In this direction men who have come down from the Public Schools and the Universities can help outside school hours in boys' clubs. Girls' clubs are no less needed. Then, in Newcastle, with its ample open spaces, there is great opportunity for the organising of boys' games, for coaching boys in cricket and football, and in refereeing. Similar work might be done for girls' games. In play centres the games

themselves could be organised. Through genial
contact of this kind, unselfishness, good feeling,
and a right spirit are induced.

Organisations like the Guild of Help, where
actual friendly work among the poor is coupled
with the study of problems of poverty and economics, provide a splendid sphere of work for men
and women of culture. And for practical work
among poor children the activities of the Poor
Children's Holiday Association and the Rescue
Association respectively offer great opportunity.

The Workers' Education Association, Adult
Schools, good debating societies, particularly local
' Houses of Parliament,' where vital subjects can
be discussed sanely and with good temper, provide
splendid openings for work. And if some of our
trained men from good schools and Universities
were to join Friendly Societies as ordinary paying
members, they would learn much and be able to
understand the worker better. The New City will
be built up, not on equality of circumstances, but
on intelligent, sympathetic fellow-feeling between
all classes. One of our keenest workers amongst
the worst characters in Newcastle—people whom
he loves and is gradually raising—believes that our
policemen ought to be University men. There is
good sense behind the apparent absurdity. University settlements could prove centres for the
dissemination of wise and considered views and
steady judgment in matters of national and inter-
national importance.

There is a popular delusion that in social work
such as I have suggested a person descends to a
lower level there to radiate complacently the genial
light and heat of a superior being. Actual workers

are under no such misapprehension, but know that they themselves are the most benefited. For they realise how much stronger than themselves in the fundamental virtues are many of the working men and women they meet, with whom they will be privileged, if they are wise enough and modest enough, to build up a real friendship.

Parents of all classes ought increasingly to recognise that great sacrifices of time and inclination made by them in order to secure for their children sound example and wholesome discipline and teaching in the home are repaid a hundredfold to themselves, and to their city and nation. Undoubtedly one of the social problems of the day is the carelessness of the parent. The education of the parent is almost as pressing a need as that of the children.

It is impossible in dealing with remedial agencies altogether to avoid mention of the part which definitely religious teaching and organisation can play. It is the custom nowadays to consider social remedies apart from definite religion, but so long as man is an erring creature, and so long as social problems arise mainly from his errors and his misdeeds, it will be necessary to maintain something more than a moral standard. No system of education can, in my opinion, be called complete which does not appeal not only to the sense of right, and honour, and truth, and fair dealing with one's neighbour, but to the conscience and the instinct of worship. Entirely apart from sectarianism there can surely be some form of religious expression, some common method of worship. The golden rule, the simple commandment, ' Thou shalt love the Lord thy God with all thy heart, and with all thy soul, and with all thy mind, and with all thy strength, and thy neighbour as thyself,' is neither abstract nor partisan. At any rate an education which can find no place for that reverence and awe which arise from, let us say, the mystery of death and life—common experiences for every scholar— fills one with misgivings.

Printed by T. and A. CONSTABLE, Printers to His Majesty
at the Edinburgh University Press

INDEX

L

Printed by T. and A. CONSTABLE, Printers to His Majesty
at the Edinburgh University Press

The List of Titles
in the Garland Series

9. Edward Cadbury, M. Cécile Matheson and George Shann. **Women's Work and Wages.** London, 1906.

10. Arnold Freeman. **Boy Life and Labour. The Manufacture of Inefficiency.** London, 1914.

11. Edward G. Howarth and Mona Wilson. **West Ham. A Study in Social and Industrial Problems.** London, 1907.

12. B.L. Hutchins. **Women in Modern Industry.** London, 1915.

13. M. Loane. **From Their Point of View.** London, 1908.

14. J. Ramsay Macdonald. **Women in the Printing Trades. A Sociological Study.** London, 1904.

15. C.F.G. Masterman. **From the Abyss. Of Its Inhabitants by One of Them.** London, 1902.

16. L.C. Chiozza Money. **Riches and Poverty.** London, 1906.

17. Richard Mudie-Smith, Ed. **Handbook of the "Daily News" Sweated Industries' Exhibition.** London, 1906.

18. Edward Abbott Parry. **The Law and the Poor.** London, 1914.

19. Alexander Paterson. **Across the Bridges. Or Life by the South London River-side.** London, 1911.

20. M.S. Pember-Reeves. **Round About a Pound a Week.** London, 1913.

21. B. Seebohm Rowntree. **Poverty. A Study of Town Life.** London, 1910 (2nd ed.).

22. B. Seebohm Rowntree and Bruno Lasker. **Unemployment. A Social Study.** London, 1911.

23. B. Seebohm Rowntree and A.C. Pigou. **Lectures on Housing.** Manchester, 1914.

24. C.E.B. Russell. **Social Problems of the North.** London and Oxford, 1913.

25. Henry Solly. **Working Men's Social Clubs and Educational Institutes.** London, 1904.

26. E.J. Urwick, Ed. **Studies of Boy Life in Our Cities.** London, 1904.

27. Alfred Williams. **Life in a Railway Factory.** London, 1915.

28. [Women's Co-operative Guild]. **Maternity. Letters from Working-Women, Collected by the Women's Co-operative Guild with a preface by the Right Hon. Herbert Samuel, M.P.** London, 1915.

29. Women's Co-operative Guild. **Working Women and Divorce. An Account of Evidence Given on Behalf of the Women's Co-operative Guild before the Royal Commission on Divorce.** London, 1911.

   bound with Anna Martin. **The Married Working Woman. A Study.** London, 1911.